Polar Frontiers

A Background Book on the Arctic,
the Antarctic, and
Mankind

Polar Frontiers

*A Background Book on the Arctic,
the Antarctic, and
Mankind*

BY RICHARD B. LYTTLE

Parents' Magazine Press • New York

Each Background Book is concerned with the broad spectrum of people, places and events affecting the national and international scene. Written simply and clearly, the books in this series will engage the minds and interest of people living in a world of great change.

G590
.L9

GL

Copyright © 1972 by Richard B. Lyttle
Printed in the United States of America

Maps by Donald Pitcher

Library of Congress Cataloging in Publication Data

Lyttle, Richard B.
  Polar frontiers.

  (A Background book)
  Bibliography: p.
  1. Polar regions—History. 2. Eskimos. I. Title
G580.L9   919.8   72-741
ISBN 0-8193-0600-2
ISBN 0-8193-0601-0 (lib. bdg.)

This book is for my mother,
Florence B. Lyttle

Acknowledgments

For help with research and organization, many thanks are due Laura Walters, Grace Miller, Florence B. Lyttle, Peter Rose, Arthur E. Gordon, Don Keown, and C. Richard Roth. I am particularly grateful for the encouragement and support of Barthold Fles, while the debt owed Edward F. Dolan, Jr. for his generous assistance can never be repaid. Finally, and most important, I give thanks to my wife, Jean, whose patience, understanding, and love have made this book possible.

Contents

Introduction

To the Ends of the Earth

THE ARCTIC AND the Antarctic challenge us. They are frontiers, not in the old, Wild West sense of the word, but frontiers in man's search for knowledge and in his quest for self-betterment.

A rugged individualist may have had his place in western expansion, but in the polar regions he is a threat. Here, more than any place on earth, man must practice trust and cooperation. Here, too, man must curb his restless urge to tamper with nature. He must recognize that human values are more important than material values. To succeed, sometimes even to survive, man must draw upon the best that is in him. From the historical view, he must improve.

The Arctic and the Antarctic are frontiers indeed. They are cold frontiers. How cold? On August 24, 1960, Soviet scientists at Vostok, eight hundred miles from the South Pole, recorded —126.9° F, the earth's coldest known surface temperature. The Arctic does not get nearly as cold, but sub-zero readings can usually be expected nine months of the year.

The sun's rays strike the earth's equatorial region at right angles, producing more heat there than can be lost through radiation. The condition is reversed at the poles. At a low angle, the sun cannot provide enough heat to replace what is lost. The imbalance in world heating sets ocean currents and winds in motion. These, in turn, govern weather and climate. A change in polar temperatures could change the lives of every man, woman, and child on earth.

In addition to cold, the Arctic and Antarctic hold another feature in common. Both are beautiful, often starkly so. The air is clear and dazzling, and the light of the sun or moon angling through this air does strange and marvelous things. Rings often appear around the sun and the rings are some-times studded with images of the sun. Polar mirages misled explorers time and again. Men charted land where no land existed. During the winter night, the polar skies flash and shimmer with yellow, green, orange, and red lights. The struggle to understand the cause of these spectacular displays did not end until the middle of the twentieth century.

Beyond the cold and the beauty, the Arctic and the Ant-arctic are striking in their differences.

The Arctic is an ocean of 5,540,000 square miles, with an

average depth of 4,200 feet, an ocean nearly enclosed by the shores of continents. The Antarctic is a continent of 5,100,000 square miles, with an average height of 6,000 feet, a continent surrounded by oceans. (See maps, pages 10 and 142.)

With the exception of a few glaciers that feed into it, the Arctic Ocean's cover of ice is frozen sea water. Sea ice also forms around Antarctica, but the spectacular bergs, some up to one hundred miles long, come from the ice shelves of its two sheltered seas.

While lichens and a few species of insect make up the only permanent biology of the Antarctic continent, the shores of the Arctic support many plants and animals. Human beings have survived in the Arctic for thousands of years. There is no evidence that man ever lived on Antarctica. The few scientists and workers who live there now are transients, being replaced nearly always by new crews each year.

The Arctic is far more accessible than the Antarctic. Man has reached the North Pole on everything from dog sledges to submarines and snowmobiles. Commercial and military planes fly over or close to the North Pole frequently. Until America established its scientific station at the South Pole in 1957, only ten men had ever stood there, and five of them did not survive the journey home. There have been about twenty tourist excursions to the shores of Antarctica. It will never become a resort. The time and money needed to get there will prevent that. On the other hand, northern tourism increases yearly. Alaska today counts the tourist business as its fourth most important industry.

The main reason for the difference in attraction has already been mentioned. Water retains heat better than land. The Arctic is thus warmer than the Antarctic. Record Arctic cold, in fact —90.4° F, is claimed by two neighboring villages in East Siberia, five hundred miles inland from the Arctic shore. A second reason why the Arctic attracts more interest is that the continents which form its shores are home for 90 percent of the earth's population. The Arctic today is similar to the Mediterranean of Roman times. The major world powers surround it. Those nations holding hostile intent toward another see the Arctic as a battleground.

The Antarctic, on the other hand, lies seven hundred miles from the closest other continent. Between the southern tips of Africa and South America and Antarctica rage the stormiest waters of the world. In isolation, the Antarctic has been left in peace, a peace that the major powers have sought to preserve by formal pact. Today, many look upon the Antarctic Treaty as the chief hope in guiding mankind to world peace.

Both the Arctic and the Antarctic, however, are part of a global controversy that could shatter peace. Who has rights to the ocean? In 1971, Iceland announced its intention to extend its claim to exclusive, off-shore fishing rights from twelve to fifty miles. The new policy was to take effect in 1972.

Some South American nations make even greater claims. Without agreement, violence may erupt among world fishing fleets. Minerals are involved, too. Large nations, such as the United States and Russia, claim ownership for oil and other minerals in the continental shelves surrounding their extensive shores. Smaller nations, with little or no shoreline, dispute such claims. This debate has special significance in the Arctic where shallow seas extend up to three hundred miles from the shore.[1]

Still another difference between the polar regions is that of seasonal variation. Arctic summer, though brief, brings a spectacular surge of life. Migratory birds fill the air with mating calls. The tundra literally blooms with flowers of long dormant plants. Animals wake from hibernation and rush into the business of feeding, mating, and rearing young. It is not all pleasant. Clouds of mosquitoes and gnats can drive an unprotected man to insanity. And sometimes it actually gets too hot—over 100° F occasionally.

Both polar regions have many islands. For a time it was thought that Antarctica was not a continent but an ice-covered archipelago. We know now that the high ice plateau, shaped like a half moon with its bulging side toward the Indian Ocean, rests on land well above sea level. The straight side of the half moon is defined by the Transantarctic Mountains, a range cutting from the west side of the Ross Sea almost to the east side of the Weddell Sea. The two seas and their ice shelves are separated by another high plateau called Marie Byrd Land and by the mountainous Antarctic Peninsula, an extension of South America's Andes. It is off the peninsula that most of the Antarctic islands are grouped. The South Shetland and South Orkney islands as well as South Georgia Island served as steps that marked the way to sealing grounds and discovery in the early days of the last century.

The Arctic islands are generally larger. Svalbard, Franz Josef Land, Novaya Zemlya, Severnaya Zemla, and Novosibirskiye Islands provide a pattern of outposts halfway around the Arctic Ocean. Iceland, Greenland, and the Arctic Archipelago—that maze of islands and sea channels—all have a long history of exploration.

Generalizations about the polar regions can be misleading. Alaskans are always quick to point out that the temperature at Kodiak Island has never dropped lower than $-16°$ F which puts it on a par with Little Rock, Arkansas. We have already seen that the coldest temperatures are not at the poles.

The ends of the earth have many boundaries, but the most common are the Arctic and Antarctic circles at $66\frac{1}{2}°$ north latitude and $66\frac{1}{2}°$ south latitude respectively. During the longest day of summer in the northern hemisphere, a man at the Arctic Circle will never see the sun set. On the longest day of winter, he will never see the sun rise. The same is true for the southern hemisphere summer and winter. These circles are defined by the tip of the earth's axis $23\frac{1}{2}°$ from the plane of its orbit around the sun. They are arbitrary boundaries. The northern third of the Antarctic Peninsula lies outside the Antarctic Circle. Much of Norway's coast within the Arctic Circle is warmed by the Atlantic current and enjoys much milder weather than Iceland, which lies just outside the Arctic Circle in the center of south-flowing polar currents.

Botanists like to use the tree line as their Arctic boundary. It wanders across the continents, sometimes above and sometimes below the Arctic Circle. North of the tree line, no trees except for the ground-hugging Arctic willow can grow. In the Antarctic, where no trees grow, such a boundary is, of course, meaningless, but the Antarctic has some natural limits of its own, all of which move with the seasons. The "shore" of the continent moves. In summer, much of the rocky coast is exposed, but in winter the surrounding water freezes, extending the boundary several hundred miles to the north and doubling the ice surface of the Antarctic. When this sea ice breaks up, off-shore winds drive floes far from land to form a halo of ice surrounding the continent. For explorers, this pack formed a very real boundary; sometimes in years of heavy ice, it was a barrier. Just beyond the pack lies yet another boundary that rings the continent. This is the zone little more than seven miles wide where the cold polar waters meet the warm waters of the Atlantic, Pacific, and Indian oceans. The Antarctic Convergence, as it is called, is a boundary of life, for here the sea surges with vital minerals that support a profusion of microscopic plants and animals which support, in turn, huge, floating herds of crustaceans. The crustaceans, mostly a small shrimp called krill, attract schools of hungry fish and whales, seals, and penguins by the thousands.

Although they never approached the polar regions, early Greek scholars managed to picture an earth with a north and south pole. In attempting to describe these regions, the Greeks gave them their names. The Greek word ἀρκτικός (Arktikos) means "near the Bear or polar constellation," what we more commonly call the Big Dipper today. From this adjective Arctic and Antarctic evolved.

This book will describe many polar studies ranging from archaeology to magnetism, from solar radiation to biology. None of the studies can be called complete; most grow more complex as work continues. Here we can do little more than describe the current status of such studies and hope that the reader's curiosity will be aroused. The book gives the high points of polar exploration and tells the story of whaling and sealing in both regions. The division of the book into two parts may at times seem arbitrary. In several cases, a single explorer's career took him to both the Arctic and the Antarctic. Whaling in both regions has followed the same tragic course. Modern science, of course, cannot be contained in any boundaries or divisions if man's mind is to grow. To organize the book, however, division was necessary. So we begin with a look into the Arctic's distant past.

PART ONE

The Arctic

Sea of Okhotsk

Kamchatka Peninsula

Magadan

S i b e r i a U. S.

Y A K U T

Lena R.

R E G S

Kolyma R.

ARCTIC CIRCLE 66½° N.

Anadyr R.

Bering I.

Attu I.

Shemya I.

Kiska I.

Amchitka I.

Novosibirskiye I (New Siberian Isl.

A r c t

Wrangel I.

Bering Sea

Adak I.

Atka I.

Aleutian Islands

Chukchi Sea

St. Lawrence I.

Bering Str.

Cape Krusenstern

Pribilof Is.

Umnak I.

Dutch Harbor

Unalaska I.

Nunivak I.

Nome

Norton Sd.

Seward Peninsula

Cape Denbigh

Kobuk R.

Point Barrow

Prudhoe Bay

NO MA PO

McClu

ALASKA

Yukon R.

Old Crow R.

Banks I.

Prince of Wa Str.

Clear

Cook Inlet

Kennedy Channel

Anchorage

Kodiak I.

Valdez

Cordova

Kayak I.

St. Elias Mts.

Gulf of Alaska

Dawson

Klondike R.

Mackenzie R.

Norman Wells

Pacific Ocean

Whitehorse

Great Bear Lake

Yellowknife

Pine Point

Great Slav Lake

C A N

ARCTIC
REGIONS

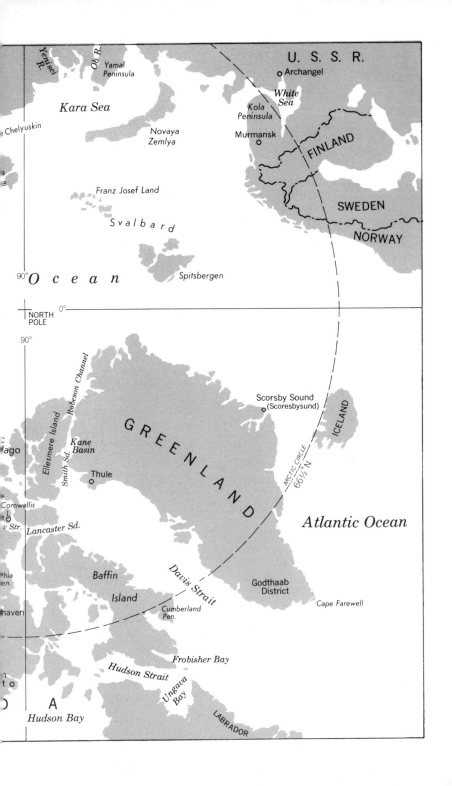

I

Ancient Men of the North

IN THE SUMMER of 1940, while still a student at the University of Alaska, J. Louis Giddings, Jr., explored the valley of the Kobuk River, searching for ruins of Eskimo houses. He found several, and using a new tool of archaeology—tree-ring dating—he determined that the timbers in some of the homes had been cut more than five hundred years ago.

Late in the season, Giddings came to ruins at a place called Onion Portage. Wild onions bloomed on a grassy knoll at a big bend in the river. Here natives coming up the river would carry their canoes or kayaks over the knoll, saving themselves five miles of hard paddling. Eskimos told Giddings that hunters had camped at Onion Portage for many, many years. It was an ideal spot to wait for the caribou migrations. Giddings saw the depressions of several house pits. They seemed older than any he had seen so far, but summer ends early in northwest Alaska and he did not get a chance to dig at Onion Portage until the following year, when he and a fellow archaeology student returned to the Kobuk.

The summer of 1941 was the wettest Eskimos of the region could remember. Rain choked the river to a record high, but on the knoll at Onion Portage Giddings and his friend, aided by enthusiastic natives, managed to excavate four house pits.

Through the ages, Arctic people built into the earth, excavating two or three feet below the surface of the ground. The ditch of the entrance tunnel was roofed with timbers and mounded earth. Half walls were built around the living chamber. The walls, and perhaps a central brace or two, supported the roof timbers. Building into the ground gave good insulation against cold, and it was a practical method in a land of few trees. When the walls and braces collapsed, the pit remained as lasting evidence of an Arctic home.

In the muddy floor of a house pit at Onion Portage, Giddings found tiny blades of flint a quarter inch wide and no longer than a pin. These were startling. At that time, microblades, as they are called, had been discovered at only one other place in North America. That was at the Campus Site at University of Alaska in Fairbanks, and archaeologists were unable to explain them. Microblades had always been considered an Old World phenomenon produced by Stone Age craftsmen of Asia who lived from eight to twelve thousand years ago. How did the small flints reach the floor of an Eskimo house just a few hundred years old?

The question was to nag Giddings for twenty years. He suspected that the blades may have been unearthed from a deeper level. The flints would have been saved as a curiosity by the early Eskimos. To prove such a notion, however, he would have to dig again at Onion Portage. His return was long delayed.

World War II suspended archaeology. It was not until the summer of 1948 when Giddings, his student days behind him, returned to the Arctic. He went, not to Onion Portage, but to a more accessible site on Cape Denbigh in Norton Sound, an arm of the Bering Sea. It was well south of Onion Portage, but here again Giddings found microblades, hundreds of them, the biggest collection yet seen in the Arctic. It was an archaeological gold mine, and it proved the existence in the far north of a culture that related closely to one that once flourished in the Gobi Desert of Central Asia where similar microblades had been found.

Since the Cape Denbigh find, microblades have been discovered in other sites from Alaska across Canada to Greenland. The people who made them, some archaeologists say, were direct ancestors of the Eskimos. If so, the Eskimos long ago lost the art of making the blades. Microblade people set the tiny flints into bone or wooden spear points. The flints opened wounds and the many cuts hastened bleeding.

Giddings's next work brought more light on the pageant of ancient man in the Arctic. Diggers in the far north had long been frustrated by the lack of stratified soil. Permafrost and tundra did not have the layered silt that gave archaeologists in lower latitudes a working chronicle. There, the older relics were buried deeper than the more recent. In the Arctic a modern spear point might be found side-by-side with one made a thousand years before.

At Cape Krusenstern west of Onion Portage on the Chukchi coast, Giddings found a series of 115 beach ridges. The youngest was lapped by waves. The oldest lay more than a mile inland against a rocky cliff. The series of ridges were created by a rising coast. As the heavy ice of the Ice Age melted, freeing the land of its burden, the land rose. On nearly every ridge, Giddings found house ruins and spear and lance points of flint, and by figuring the age of each successive beach, he could date the finds. On one beach, he again discovered microblades. They had been left there by hunters three thousand years ago.

The most amazing revelation of the Krusenstern beaches, however, was the variety they revealed. There were people who lived almost entirely on caribou. Could they have been ancestors of American Indians who even today prefer land hunting to marine hunting and fishing? There were some people who lived almost entirely on whales. Some hunted seals. Other carved wood, still others ivory. Some made pottery. What had become of these people?

Prior to the finds at Krusenstern, no one suspected the Arctic had ever had such a diversity of Stone Age people.

On top of the rocky cliff above the oldest beach, Giddings and his helpers found a crude chopper so old that chemical change had softened the stone. Giddings guessed it might be six thousand years old.

The work at Cape Krusenstern took several summers. Giddings became a professor at Brown University. He learned more and more of ancient man, and he grew to know and like the Kotzebue Eskimos who worked with him at the cape. They had a legend that explained microblades. The little flints were so small, the Eskimos said, that they had to be made by small people. These gnome-like creatures lived deep in the ground, which explained why no one saw them. Giddings suspected that such a tale may have been started by Eskimos who accidentally discovered microblades and left the microblades on the floor of a recent house like the one he excavated at Onion Portage. Giddings returned to the site on the Kobuk on July 5, 1961.

His colleagues often credited him with an uncanny instinct in knowing where to dig, but it was logic and experience that brought Giddings back to Onion Portage. He lost little time in chopping away the tangle of wild rose bushes that covered the site of his twenty-year-old dig. Then he went to work with a shovel. At once he turned up a dark mixture of charcoal and bone. These were leg bones of caribou broken into short lengths. Before the Eskimos, Giddings decided, Indians had camped at Onion Portage, for it was an Indian practice to break and boil bones for a rich marrow broth. Within a few hours, stone and obsidian points, knives and scrapers came to light to give further evidence that the level was Indian. Were there other levels below? Later in the summer, with more helpers and a greater expanse of thawed earth, Giddings probed deeper. In careful hands the trowels scraped through layer after layer of soil, layer after layer of relics left by Stone Age man. Onion Portage was indeed the answer to an archaeologist's dream. Giddings concentrated

on the new find. For three summers, he led the work at
Onion Portage. Then in 1964, at age 55, he died of injuries
from a traffic accident.

Work at Onion Portage was far from finished, but Giddings had learned enough to support new theories on Arctic
man. For one thing, he showed that the concept of one-way,
land-bridge migration from the Old World to the New
World at the close of the Ice Age was a gross simplification.
The land link between Siberia and Alaska lasted thousands
of years. Migrations moved both ways. And while the land
bridge certainly played an important part in these migrations,
there also may have been large movements across open water
by boat and across the ice of the frozen sea before and after
the land bridge existed. The exchange of customs, skills, even
language, said Giddings, was circumpolar.

Studies and discoveries since Giddings's death all tend to
support his ideas, We know today that the land bridge, now
beneath the shallow Chukchi and Bering seas, was a 1,300-
mile wide plain of tundra that existed from ten thousand to
twenty-five thousand years ago. Then much of the water of
the world's oceans was land-trapped in the ice sheets.
Strangely, though the continental ice reached far south,
much of Alaska, particularly the valley of the Yukon River,
was ice free. Growth along the Yukon was lush, almost sub-
tropical, ideal for both man and the animals he hunted.

Recent finds strongly suggest that Stone Age hunters
came to North America before the land bridge existed. In
1967, C. R. Harrington of the National Museum of Canada
found a bone pick and a bone scraper among skeletal remains of bison, horses, camels, giant moose, and giant beaver

on the Old Crow River in the Canadian Yukon. These animals roamed the Arctic forty thousand years ago. Much farther south in the Calico Mountains not far from San Bernardino, California, diggers under the supervision of Louis S. B. Leakey of South African archaeological fame, have found a fire hearth and stone tools in alluvial soil laid down fifty thousand to one hundred thousand years ago. These finds make the land bridge seem a pathway for late-comers.

Continued digging at Onion Portage showed that migration was a tradition of Stone Age man for thousands of years. Douglas D. Anderson, a former student of Giddings, now supervising the dig on the Kobuk, has found tools that were left by people camping at Onion Portage at least thirteen thousand years ago. This lowest level yet reached in the sand and clay, twelve feet below ground level, has yielded micro-blades and many stone tools, including a disc-shaped scraper. Similar scrapers have been found only on the shores of Lake Baikal in central Siberia where hunters camped from twelve thousand to fifteen thousand years ago.

Higher up, in a level laid down about eight thousand years ago, Anderson and his associates found a sparse scattering of microblades and scrapers, not much different from the oldest finds. At this level, however, the relics are scarce, suggesting that the people who left them stayed very briefly at Onion Portage, perhaps no longer than the caribou season each year. Above this sparse layer, sterile ground shows no occupancy for two thousand years. Why? No one can yet say. Next, at eight feet below the surface, is a level rich in stone spear and arrow points, points that have been notched to hold bindings, the typical Indian-head design. These finds are entirely different from those of the lower levels, and Anderson believes they were left by ancestors of Indians who moved north into Alaska with the warmer climate that followed the Ice Age.[2] There are no microblades in these deposits, but higher up, about six feet below the surface, microblades appear again. This new level represents the culture that left small blades throughout much of the Arctic.

In a still higher level, as we have seen, are relics of Indians who boiled bones for soup and, above this, the tools of recent ancestors of the Eskimos.

A long-held theory had it that man was driven to the northern barrens by his enemies. This notion has been generally discarded. Today, most students of early man believe the occupation of the Far North was voluntary. The Stone-Age hunters depended on animals and followed them into the north as the Ice Age came to an end. As the ice sheets melted, the animals ranged farther and farther into the Arctic. So did man.

The Arctic once had a larger native population than today, and the character of the people has changed greatly in the past hundred years. Among the seventy thousand Eskimos of Alaska, Canada, and Greenland, a pure-blooded native would be hard to find today. The blood of European and American whalers, even of Vikings, is liberally spread through the current population. The Yukaghirs, Chukchi, Koryaks, and Samoyeds represent less than 4 percent of today's population of Siberia, and there are Cossacks in the ancestry of many. Even the Lapps of the Scandinavian Peninsula, now numbering no more than thirty-two thousand are intermarrying with Norwegians, Swedes, and Russians. In addition, customs have been forgotten. Traditions have been lost. Before the influence of modern civilization reached the far north, however, the scattered tribes followed customs and traditions that showed remarkable similarities throughout the Arctic.

2

Arctic People

THE LAPPS BELIEVED that giving a newborn child the name of a recently dead and respected relative would put the spirit of the relative into the child. Many Siberian natives and the Eskimos followed the same practice. Both Lapps and Eskimos used the skin of fawns killed in August for inner clothing. All across the Arctic, before the arrival of missionaries, the spiritual life was based on shamanism. Each village had its respected shaman, or medicine man, who could cure the ill, foretell the future, and defend against evil spirits. Often, the shaman had to go into a trance to perform his magic. Eskimo and Lapp shamans both used ceremonial drums to assist in attaining the state of trance.

Surface examination of the traditions suggests a common origin for all peoples of the far north, but we know this was not the case. Though origins are much debated, the Lapps probably worked north from central Europe, following the reindeer which they at first hunted and later herded. Lapps, because they needed speed in following their herds, were first among all peoples to use the ski. While other natives of the north did not adopt the ski, the snowshoes used by Lapps, Siberians, and Eskimos are nearly alike.

Among the Siberian natives, the Tungus spread from the steppe region of Asia across Siberia and into Japan. The Yakuts and Samoyeds, also from the steppes, came north later to possess much of the Tungus's domain. The Yakuts, whose language resembles Turkish, have retained words for such things as camels and lions after living for generations in a land where no camels or lions exist. More easterly tribes of Siberia—the Chukchi, Yukaghirs, and Koryaks—probably originated in Mongolia, perhaps sharing their ancestry with the Eskimo. The Chukchi and Eskimo languages are so similar that natives of the eastern tip of Asia and the western tip of America have little trouble understanding each other.

New theories on Eskimo origin keep appearing. The Soviet anthropologist S. I. Rudenko recently suggested that Eskimos came from the Melanesian Islands of the South Pacific.[3] These islanders, Rudenko declared, were the only Stone Age people who developed sufficient skill with small boats and harpoons to meet the challenge of the north. The islanders migrated to the Arctic by way of mainland Asia and the islands of Japan, according to Rudenko. This might explain the similarity of certain stone implements found in Japan and Alaska, but it ignores the Eskimo birth spot, a blue mark at the base of the spine. The only other babies with such a spot born today are those of Mongolia.

Despite the debate and new theories, it seems clear that the natives of the north did not have a common origin, and the customs and traditions held in common were spread through hundreds of years of circumpolar migrations just as Giddings suggested.

Unfortunately, recent changes in the north force one to speak of the unique lives of the natives in the past tense. Civilization has come to the Arctic. Much of what we know today of the old ways comes from the reports of explorers who marveled at the ability of primitive peoples to adapt to a harsh environment. Part of the ability involved a remarkable physical adjustment. Yakuts, according to early Siberian explorers, would strip to the skin even when the temperature stood at —60° F and go to sleep in the snow with no more than a loose covering of their clothes and a small fire to warm them. They could sleep during a storm, even as snowflakes collected on their bare skin.

But just as remarkable to explorers was the resourcefulness and skill shown by northern man. Far north of the tree line, where scrub willows and driftwood are rare, the Eskimo hunter learned to make shafts for his weapons by joining together short lengths of bone. Kayaks and sledges were often framed with willow sticks and bone. When these materials were lacking, the Eskimo could still make a sledge by molding wet skins into the shape desired. When the skins froze hard, the Eskimo had a sledge that might last all winter.

Rather than fight nature, the Eskimo learned to turn it to his advantage. The snow igloo was the classic example. Most Eskimos of the north Canadian coast could cut snow blocks and put up a snug shelter in less than thirty minutes. Necessity has forced some hunters to retain the skill to this day. When sudden blizzards hit, shelter means survival.

Eskimo hunting methods combined skill and patience. In winter, the hunter would search the sea ice for a seal breathing hole. When a hole was found, the hunter would stand above it with spear poised, waiting. Often the wait lasted for hours. Many times the hunt would fail. Seals, which must come up for air every ten to twenty minutes, maintain several holes through the ice. Chance might not take the seal to the hole the hunter had found, or a slight shadow or unusual noise could warn the seal of danger. In summer, hunters caught seals with nets or stalked them behind portable screens of skin.

Many natives of the north managed to live almost entirely on the elusive seal. The seal's skin provide clothing, dog harness, fishing nets, and bindings for many uses. The blubber burned in oil lamps gave both heat and light. Seal meat was nourishing food, and in cold weather it could be stored for months without spoiling. Bones provided building material for many uses. Even the teeth of the seal were used to edge scrapers and other tools. Nothing was wasted. Intestines made waterproof parkas or food storage bags. What a man and his family did not eat, the dogs did.

Those who hunted the walrus found many uses for the long ivory tusks. They could be carved for spear points, knives, and scrapers. Even needles could be made from ivory. The thick skin of the walrus provided tough but easy to

preserve food. It also made the best shoe soles. The best
sewing thread came from the sinew in the back of the
narwhal, although the hind legs of the caribou had sinew
that could serve nearly as well. Narwhals, with their long,
unicorn-like horn, also provided ivory as well as meat and
blubber.

In summer, the Eskimo and his family gathered bird eggs
and berries. Many natives used the down-covered skin of
birds for warm undershirts. Tiny auks provided a rare
delicacy reported by the Dane Peter Freuchen, who wrote of
the Eskimos of Smith Sound, the most northern people of
the world.[4] Early in this century, Freuchen and Knud Ras-
mussen established a trading post at Thule in northwest
Greenland, present site of a United States Air Force Base.

Preparation of an auk dinner in Freuchen's honor took
time. It was managed by a native gourmet of high reputation.
First the auks were collected by men who draped nets over
a cliff where the birds nested. Next a seal was killed and its
carcass hollowed out, leaving just the skin and an inner
lining of blubber. Then the auks, feathers and all, were
stuffed into the seal, the opening sewn shut and the entire
package buried beneath the floor of the gourmet's house. The
dinner was allowed to ripen several months. When the day
of the banquet arrived, eager hands raised the stuffed seal.
Rancid fat, Freuchen reported, had worked wondrous things
on the tiny auks. The crunchy birds, he said, provided some
of the tastiest morsels he had ever sampled. But Freuchen
also explained that his host would have thought it an un-
forgivable insult if anyone had refused the feast.

The Eskimo developed many fishing methods. Barbed
spears, nets, traps, and baited hooks served to land fish. The

catch could be preserved by drying or freezing. For some natives, fish made up nearly 50 percent of the diet. Fishing remains an important source of food, particularly where natives retain exclusive fishing rights on Arctic streams and rivers.

The most important land animal for the Eskimo was the caribou. In addition to meat, the caribou bone and antlers provided material for tools and the skins, when sewn together, made a fine tent cloth for the summer home. Caribou skin, of course, was also used extensively throughout the Arctic for clothing. Stomach contents from the caribou, usually partially digested lichen, was an Eskimo delicacy. In time of starvation, Eskimos ate caribou droppings to stay alive.

Starvation was a powerful factor in the development of the hardy, resourceful Eskimo. It was always a threat, and when seal hunting failed or a fish run was delayed by late thaw, only the most skillful hunter managed to keep himself and his family alive. The weak and inept died. Explorers heard tales of men and women who killed their children or aged parents in lean years to save them from suffering and improve the chances of survival for the productive members of a family. The aged, who could no longer hunt or perform other useful duties, often welcomed death even in good years. At the height of a party, when the Eskimo's house rang with laughter, a man or his wife might take a stout thong and strangle an old parent who had seen too many years. This was done at the request of the parent who wanted to die at a moment of happiness.

Such stories are hard to reconcile with the Eskimo's reputation as a family man. Even today, few people cherish and love their children and respect and honor their elders more than the Eskimo. Parents do not strike a child.

The Eskimo household was a busy place. The woman spent many hours making clothing for her husband and children. So important was warm, well-made clothing, that the success of a man's marriage would often be judged by the quality of clothing he wore. Arctic clothing, varying little between Asia and North America, follows a loose-fitting design which allows much air circulation around the body. The only close-fitting areas are over the shoulders and around the neck and head, a design that prevents escape of rising body heat.

In winter, Eskimos and other Arctic natives put on a double layer of skins. In summer weather, a single layer was enough, sometimes too much under continuous sun, but the hide parka and trousers were necessary armament against gnats and mosquitoes. Before starting to cut and sew, an Eskimo woman would spend hours chewing the seal or caribou hides to soften them. Then, without any pattern to guide her, she would cut the skins with her flint knife. Stitching, despite the ivory needles and sinew thread, would be fine, just as evenly spaced as machine sewing. Rarely would the job have to be reworked because of poor fit.

The bachelor Eskimo was to be pitied. If he could not get second-hand clothing from a married friend or find some man's wife who would sew for him in exchange for food or skins, he had to fumble at making his own clothes. These male compositions more often than not brought ridicule, something few Eskimos could long endure.

Because the animal oil fuel was precious, few Eskimos ate more than one cooked meal a day. Most meat was eaten raw.

"Eskimo" comes from an Indian word meaning "eater of raw meat." Many Eskimos, however, called themselves *Innuit* which means "people of the land."

By our standards, some of the Eskimo hunting methods were cruel. The spring trap, for instance, brought agonizing death to the wolf. This was a slat of whalebone, sharpened at both ends, bent double, and buried in a chunk of fresh meat. The meat was allowed to freeze before being set out for the wolf. The unfortunate wolf that swallowed the meat died slowly of a punctured stomach after the thawing morsel released the sprung bone. When he used the spring trap, however, the Eskimo was not being deliberately cruel. For him, it would have been cruelty to let his family die of starvation when a little ingenuity could save them. Wolf meat might not be as good as seal, but it did sustain life.

The rigors of the Arctic, one might suppose, would make those who struggled for existence there selfish and mean and suspicious of strangers. Nothing could be further from the truth. Even during hard times, Eskimos were generous and happy. True, many explorers complained of thieving Eskimos, but the thieving occurred because the Eskimos believed that all property should be shared. If one man had no spear, it was his right to borrow from a man who had two. Soon after returning from a successful hunt, an Eskimo would usually call his neighbors to his house to share in the feast. It was an insult to refuse such invitations. Even wives, as important as they were to a man's existence, might be loaned or traded. This is not to suggest promiscuity among Eskimos. Any man making advances to a woman without her husband's consent might be banished from the village for his poor manners. At the very least, he could expect mass ridicule. For the fiercely proud Eskimo, ridicule was as bad as death itself. Indeed, an Eskimo with wounded pride might languish and die.

Disputes were sometimes settled through contests of insult rather than physical violence. The antagonists would face each other and exchange taunts. Victory came to the man who caused the villagers to laugh at his adversary.

Occasionally blood feuds arose which could not be settled by mere words. If one man killed another, the victim's family was expected to avenge the death. The chain of murders, often protracted over many years, was an accepted course of events among the Eskimos. Tough justice served for the village troublemaker. The man usually had to be disposed of because he endangered the community, either through eating more than his share in time of want or habitually violating important tabus. When village leaders decided death was the only answer, they selected one among them to execute the sentence. Responsibility, however, was spread among all. It would be pointless for the man's relatives to seek revenge.

There was little warfare among the Eskimos. Meeting the necessities of life kept them too busy to organize an attack or even an effective defense. Their traditional enemy, the Indian, showed far more skill at war.

Eskimos believed in many spirits, including spirits of those recently dead. The dead had to be provided with clothing, food, and weapons for life in the other world. Otherwise their spirits might return to cause trouble. Some Eskimos believed that a hole must be chopped in the roof of a dead man's house to allow his spirit to escape.

The animals that the Eskimo hunted also had spirits. An important function of the village shaman was to keep these spirits happy. Beliefs in spirits varied from region to region, but one spirit stood out in the beliefs of Eskimos throughout Canada and Greenland. This was the sea woman, an ugly hag who lived in the bottom of the sea and ruled all the sea animals.

If a hunter used a dead man's kayak or harpoon, or if some other tabu were broken, the sea woman became angry and locked up all the animals in her house. These were the times when Eskimos returned empty-handed to their hungry wives and children. Something had to be done to appease the sea woman. The Eskimos asked their shaman for help. The shaman must go to the sea woman and talk to her. Seated before all who could crowd into his igloo, the shaman closed his eyes, beat on his drum, and went into a trance. Then he "traveled" far through the earth to the bottom of the sea where the ugly goddess lived. Early explorers who observed such rituals have described the shaman's fading chant as he spiritually departed and the return of his voice as he came back among the villagers. Often the shaman would show torn clothes and slashed skin as evidence of his encounter with the goddess. For the villagers, there was no doubt that the shaman had traveled far and done his duty. Hunting, they were sure, would soon improve.

Important as spiritism was, the success of hunting or any other venture usually rested on the quality of Eskimo equipment and his skill in using it. Take the kayak. For its purpose —transporting one man over shallow, sometimes stormy waters—the design, even today, cannot be bettered. A man with a double-headed paddle could propel this light craft rapidly and quietly over the sea. In expert hands, the kayak was remarkably seaworthy. With the bottom of his waterproof parka tied around the coaming of the cockpit, the Eskimo boatman was able to roll himself and his boat completely over without taking on water. If caught in breaking waves, a Greenland Eskimo could flip his craft to take the force of white water on the bottom of the hull. As soon as the wave passed, he would bob up and continue paddling. It was a feat of seamanship that left seasoned European mariners staring in awe and admiration. The admiration increased when it was found that these native boatmen did not know how to swim. Arctic waters discourage swimming and bathing. One bath, however, needed no water.

Norwegian explorer Roald Amundsen, who maintained a camp on King William Island in the middle of the Arctic Archipelago for two years, reported the waterless bath.[5] Invited to visit an Eskimo village, Amundsen spent the night in a snow igloo occupied by two families. When he woke in the morning, he stared in surprise. Every man, woman, and child was sitting, happily scratching and chatting in the nude. This, he learned later, was the Eskimos' traditional air bath.

Sometime far back in prehistory, Arctic natives domesticated the dog. A man's dog team was often his most prideful possession. On the winter ice and snow he could sledge from eighty to a hundred miles in one day. Dogs were also vital in the hunt. When snow covered seal breathing holes a dog was needed to scent one. In addition, if a man came upon the fresh track of a polar bear, he would release his dogs, letting them track the ice king and bring him to bay. Moving in on a cornered bear, armed with no more than a stone or ivory-tipped spear, required courage. Today, when all hunters carry rifles, the polar bear is still the most honored quarry of the Arctic. Unfortunately, as we shall see, it has become a rare quarry.

In summer, with sledges useless on the boggy tundra, dogs served as pack animals. With the help of his dogs, a man could move his family and all his possessions to summer hunting or fishing grounds.

No one can say when the Lapps first domesticated the reindeer. They have been following the practice for countless generations, getting meat, hides, and milk from their herds, even using some deer as draft animals. Reindeer of the Old World and caribou of the New are closely related, and are distinguished from other members of the deer family in that both males and females grow antlers. The caribou, however, cannot be easily tamed. Some Siberian natives started domesticating the reindeer in early times, but they are thought to have learned the skill from the Lapps. Today, under Soviet encouragement, Siberian herds have become the largest in the Arctic.

Originally, Lapps were hunters and fishermen. Long after they became herdsmen, hunting traditions were maintained. Bear hunting until recently remained a ritual with the Lapps, involving the entire community. The bear had a powerful spirit that could avenge its death. It was necessary, therefore, to spread responsibility among all the hunters for killing it.

In winter, scouts would search out and mark the bear's den. Then the big hunt would be organized. All hunters from the village would come with their spears and plant them around the den, all pointing at the spot where the bear was expected to emerge. Then one or two brave men would enter the den and chase the bear out. With luck, the angry bear would impale itself as it rushed into the open. If the bear did not escape, the hunters had a worthy trophy. They would carry the carcass proudly back to their village where women waited to perform another rite. During the hunt the women had been chewing a red bark. Each hunter on his return would be smeared with this mixture of bark and spittle as a protection against the spirit of the bear.

Lapps built a variety of houses. They made permanent homes of rock and sod around a sunken floor, much like the early Eskimo home. For hot weather, the Lapp home consisted of a circle of poles bound at the peak and covered with skins, a structure little different from the tepee of the North American Indian. Lapps, whose territory included many stands of pine and fir, also built wooden houses high at the top of poles. These served as food caches. The Samoyeds, easterly neighbors of the Lapps, built similar caches.

Not all the old ways have been lost in the Arctic. Lapps are still herding reindeer in Scandinavia, but some Lapps, particularly the young, find life easier in a fishing village or mining town. Siberian natives still hunt the walrus, but both hunters and quarry are few. In Alaska, where there are fifty-five thousand Eskimos, Indians, and Aleuts, 80 percent still follow an economy of subsistent hunting, but snowmobiles have replaced the dog sled. Wooden skiffs with outboard motors have replaced the kayak. Board and tarpaper shacks have replaced the huts of sod, rock, and driftwood.

The native of Alaska lives between two worlds, the old and the new. While caribou hides and seal meat are still vital, the portable radio, the machine-knit sweater, canned fruit, razor blades, candy, and all the other brightly packaged goods of the mainland have become important too. And where he once dominated, the native is now a minority, sometimes a bitter minority. Missionaries told him long ago that his old beliefs were wrong. Schools taught the white man's religion and customs.

In Siberia, the Cossack expansion was even tougher on the natives. Some were killed outright for a cache of hides. Others were cheated, with a few kegs of vodka, out of a wealth of ermine. Lust for drink often drove the natives to trap when they should have been doing more practical hunting to feed their families. Starvation depleted many Siberian tribes. Today, under strict management, native populations of Siberia have recovered, and we are told that the natives are sharing equally in the industrial expansion and natural resources of their land.

The story of the Caribou Eskimo of Canada's central barrens, however, is tragic. Writer Farley Mowat,[6] a specialist in the far north, tells about it in *People of the Deer*. In sixty years, the population of the Caribou Eskimo fell from two thousand to forty. The fluctuating demand for fur brought about the havoc. When the price for fox pelts was high, white traders supplied the Eskimos with guns, ammunition, and canned foods. The good times usually lasted just long enough to make the Eskimos dependent on such bounty. When the price of fur dropped, trading posts closed their doors. Ammunition for the guns could not be had, but the Eskimos had forgotten the old hunting skills. Some tried to relearn the use of spear and bow and arrow, but it took patience to stalk the deer. Few had any luck. The result was mass starvation. Meanwhile, caribou herds diminished. Prospectors burned vast stretches of the tundra to bare the ground and ease the search for minerals. This reduced the deer's range. In addition, when good times in fur trading returned, Eskimo hunters slaughtered the deer wastefully, often taking nothing but the tongue, the most desired delicacy, and leaving the rest of the animal for the wolves and the ravens.

The few men and women who survived have left the barrens and are now living in sad towns on government dole. There are other welfare communities in the Arctic created by boom and bust developments and by changes in the needs of the Eskimo's civilized brother to the south. At Rankin Inlet on the west coast of Hudson Bay, Eskimos were drawn to a nickel mine in 1957. For five years there was work for all, but then the owners abruptly closed the mine. The richest ore was gone. With few exceptions, the Eskimos, who had lost their old self-reliant ways, turned for relief to the Canadian government.

The exceptions in this grim picture are owing to men who have introduced training in various trades, mostly craft work such as ceramics, carving, and painting. Sale of such products in southern markets has provided livelihood for some Eskimos.

It is impossible to argue that modern tools and conveniences of civilization should be denied anyone. Certainly, for northern man where conditions are hard, the need for rifles, radios, packaged food, cooking ware, gas heating, electricity, and the best of building materials is great. But all too often the impact of modern life has been too sudden in the Arctic. The changes, uncontrolled and untempered, have caused the loss of much that Arctic man held good, much of self-reliance and ingenuity that might still serve as worthy examples for mankind everywhere.

3

Iceland, Greenland, and Northeast

IN ONE SENSE, the Stone Age hunters who peopled the north were the first Arctic explorers, but animal bones and flint spear points do not give a satisfactory record of discovery. Historians demand more detail—a written record.

The first such record was provided by Pytheas, a Greek navigator and geographer who voyaged north in about 325 B.C. and may have reached the Arctic Circle. Ironically, the record became history only because few men could believe what Pytheas found. His own accounts were lost, but the writing of his critics survived. Pytheas saw men and women living in a land of midnight sun, skies that flashed with strange light, furry creatures living in the sea, and he either saw or learned of the ice cap.

Pytheas lived in an age when the wisest philosophers of Greece held firmly to the belief that the world was divided into five regions. There was the middle, equatorial region so close beneath the sun that the sea boiled and the land burned. Life there was impossible. Then there were the regions of the far north and far south, both so far from the sun that all was frozen. Nothing could live in these regions either. Only the two moderate regions between the fire and the ice provided the right conditions for life.

For the Greek peasant there were other notions about the far north. There Boreas, god of the north wind, ruled, and it was also home for the hyperborean people who lived in peace and good health under eternal sunshine.

When Pytheas returned to his native Massilia, a colony on the Mediterranean coast, now the city of Marseilles, France, he quickly gained the reputation of the world's greatest liar. His stories of men mining tin on the Cornwall coast of England and of a drink these men made of honey and fermented grain were hard enough to believe, but when Pytheas told of lands even farther north, a land that stood at the edge of a frozen sea—well, that was too much. No man could go so far and return to tell about it.

Through the rest of his life and long after his death, Pytheas was ridiculed. His books burned in the fire that destroyed the library at Alexandria, but the ridicule survived. This made a poor record, and no one can be sure just how far Pytheas sailed and where his most northern land, what he called *Ultima Thule,* was located. Norwegian scholar and

explorer Fridtjof Nansen believed Pytheas sailed to a spot on
the coast of Norway in the present Trondheim district before
turning south. Canadian explorer Vilhjalmur Stefansson
argued that Iceland was Pytheas's *Ultima Thule*. Still others
said Pytheas sailed no farther than Unst, most northern of
the Shetland Islands off Scotland and that all he reported of
his *Ultima Thule* was collected secondhand from native
Shetlanders.

No historian wrote of Thule again until 825 A.D., eleven
and a half centuries after Pytheas. Then, Dicuil, an Irish
monk, told of fellow monks who sailed in tiny coracles, boats
of reeds and skins, to Iceland. Assuming this was Pytheas's
most northern landfall, Dicuil called it Thule and said there
was enough light on a summer midnight for a man to pick
the lice off his shirt. North of Thule, Dicuil said, the monks
came upon sea ice. It may have been Dicuil's account that
encouraged Irish colonization. No record can be found of this
daring venture, but we do know that when Vikings came to
Iceland late in the ninth century they found Irish living
there.

For the Norsemen, Iceland was a land of promise. Scandinavia had become overpopulated and crop production on the
rocky soil there could not keep pace with demand. Families
migrated by the thousands. Before the tenth century ended,
twenty thousand people lived on Iceland, but in this volcanic
land of snow and ice, farm land was also limited. Many
families were ready to migrate as soon as new land could be
found.

A blood feud between neighboring Iceland farmers
prompted a timely discovery. To gain peace, the governors
of Iceland decided the chief troublemaker in the dispute

should be banished for three years. His name was Erik Thorwaldson, a hot-tempered young man known to some as Erik the Red.

With his wife, two small sons, and a few loyal companions, Erik sail from Iceland toward the west in 981 A.D. His ship, an eighty-ton *knorr,* though larger than some that have since ventured into Arctic waters, offered little shelter from storm and spray and had only square sail and oars for power. Its thin, wooden planks gave scant protection against ice and rocks. Erik had no charts, no sextant, and if he carried a loadstone compass, he soon found it useless as he neared the north magnetic pole.

The east coast of Greenland had earlier been sighted by storm-blown sailors. Erik sailed down the coast to the southern tip of the island, now called Cape Farewell, and then turned north, skirting the unknown west coast. The many fjords gave ideal shelter, and Erik and his small band made several landings. Once, Erik climbed a mountain and saw another land to the west, probably the mountainous Cumberland Peninsula of Baffin Island.

Before his three-year banishment ended, Erik explored the Baffin coast as well as the western shores of Greenland, and after all his travels he decided that the fjord region with ice-free land just north of Cape Farewell offered the best region for settlement. He returned to Iceland as a land promoter, and to make his find sound inviting he called it Grønland or Greenland. Two years after his banishment ended, he sailed west again leading a fleet of twenty-five ships, but before the fleet reached Greenland, a storm struck and sank fourteen ships. The first Greenland colony was reduced to five hundred souls.

Despite the tragic beginning, the colony prospered. More families arrived from Iceland and soon a second settlement grew some three hundred miles north of the first in a region now called the Godthaab District. In summers, hunters and fishermen came from Iceland to take up temporary residence. Some went to Baffin Island to hunt caribou. In about 1003 A.D., Erik's son, Leif, voyaged south to the fabled Vinland, which scholars today believe was near the Cape Cod coast of Massachusetts. Others sailed north as far as Ellesmere Island. It was a remarkable era of Viking expansion.

History of the era is still not fully known. It still ends in mystery. After nearly five hundred years of prosperous occupation, the Greenland colonies vanished. One theory has it that the Vikings were all killed by Eskimos. Another cites the Black Plague as the villain, and another claims pirates killed or carried off the people. Stefansson, pointing to examples of "white Eskimos," said the Norsemen assimilated with the natives, interbred, and took up the life of nomadic hunters.[7] Recently, archaeologist Thomas Lee has found many stone cairns, possibly navigation marks, along the western coast of Newfoundland's Ungava Bay, and inland he has discovered a village of stone house ruins and a pond behind an earth and stone dam. There is little doubt that these are Norse ruins predating colonial times in America, but nothing found so far gives any hint of the fate of the Ungava Bay settlers.

While the Norse explorers sought new space to colonize, the explorers who followed sought trade routes. Bold navigators from Spain and Portugal pioneered the two southern routes to India and Cathay, one around Africa's Cape of Good Hope and the other around South America's storm-lashed Cape Horn. For many years, Spain and Portugal ruled the seas and restricted use of the routes to their own ships.

In the sixteenth century, Britain and Holland did not have the naval strength to force the southern routes, but merchants of both countries hungered for the jewels, silks, and spices of the Orient. They dreamed of other routes. If ships could find passage around the southern reaches of the continents, the merchants reasoned, there must be passage to the north. Such thinking dominated three centuries of Arctic exploration as daring men in frail ships challenged the unknown, searching for the fabled Northwest and Northeast passages to China.

English merchants launched the search for the Northeast Passage. Actually, a small stretch of the route had already been explored in 870 A.D. by a Viking called Ohthere who voyaged east around Scandinavia's North Cape, skirted the coast of the Kola Peninsula, and discovered the White Sea. The most profitable find on this voyage was evidently the walrus, which Ohthere called "horsewhale." He and his men killed several for the ivory of the tusks. Ohthere's report was forgotten by fellow Vikings, but he had told England's King Alfred about the journey and the record was preserved. In 1553 England sent three ships beyond North Cape. Sir Hugh Willoughby led the fleet. Richard Chancellor was second in command. All went well until a sudden storm scattered the fleet off Norway. Chancellor's ship was separated from the others. When the weather eased, he searched but failed to sight them. He decided to proceed independently.

Following the route blazed by Ohthere, Chancellor reached the White Sea and anchored in an inlet near the site of the present city of Archangel. It proved to be a safe winter haven. Willoughby was not so lucky. After the storm, he too sailed eastward, skirting the Kola coast, but he did not reach the White Sea. He put his two ships in a small bay exposed to the full thrust of winter ice. The ships were soon trapped in the ill-chosen anchorage. The following winter, curious natives boarded the ice-shrouded vessels and discovered Willoughby and all his men dead, some frozen in their bunks.

During the winter that claimed these men, Chancellor left his ship and traveled overland to Moscow. Tsar Ivan IV, eager for trade, received the Englishman warmly and the two opened negotiations. Chancellor, excited over Russian ermine and sable, hurried back to his ship and sailed for England as quickly as possible. The Orient could wait. In England, Chancellor was ordered to sail back to the White Sea at once and conclude a trade treaty with the tsar. This he did, but on his return to England, a storm again struck off Norway. When the battered ship raised the coast of Scotland it barely floated. The voyagers had to complete their trip in ship's boats. The boat carrying Chancellor swamped in the surf, and he and his wife drowned.

Chancellor's trade treaty provided foundation for the Muscovy Company which brought new wealth to England. Skippers of company ships gained valuable experience in Arctic waters and some sailed as far east as Novaya Zemlya.

The Dutch, under the leadership of Oliver Brunel, entered the White Sea trade in 1565. In one voyage Brunel's curiosity led him eastward, beyond Novaya Zemlya into the Kara Sea. Back in Holland, Brunel convinced investors he had found a new route to the Orient. He sailed again in 1582, hoping to return with a cargo of spice and silk, but he, his crew, and

his ship were never seen again. The Dutch, however, did not
lose interest in the Northeast Passage.

In the summer of 1594, merchants of Holland sent a fleet
of four ships beyond North Cape. Willem Barents, who had
skippered merchant ships and commanded sealing ventures,
led the expedition to Novaya Zemlya. There he sent two
ships to the south and two north. He stayed with the northern survey, which reached the top of the island before ice
turned it back. On rejoining his southern captains, Barents
was delighted to learn that they had crossed the Kara Sea and
sighted a headland now known as the Yamal Peninsula.

In Holland, merchants received Barents's report with equal
delight and mounted a highly ambitious expedition. It sailed
in the summer of 1595. Barents now had in his command
seven ships heavy with trade goods for the Orient. The venture failed. The passage south of Novaya Zemlya, navigated
so easily the summer before, presented a solid barrier of ice.
Barents had enough experience to know he could do but one
thing—go home. But disappointed merchants, who had never
seen pack ice and did not understand what it could do to a
wooden ship, blamed Barents for the failure.

When the next expedition sailed in 1596, Barents went not
as commander but as pilot. Captains of the two ships, Jan
Corneliszoon Rijp and Jacob van Heemskerck, shared command. Van Heemskerck showed good sense, welcoming
Barents aboard his ship and sharing his authority with the
veteran sailor, but Rijp proved headstrong and stubborn. He
ignored Barents's advice and insisted on sailing far north of
previous routes. This led to the discovery of Bear Island and
the Svalbard Archipelago, both highly significant in the development of the Dutch sealing and whaling industry that

would follow, but the northward diversion seriously delayed exploration east.

Rijp and van Heemskerck finally parted. The former soon turned for home, but the latter sailed southeast to Novaya Zemlya. Barents was pleased to find the northern tip of the island free of ice, but his pleasure soon faded. Just a few miles beyond the island, drifting floes crossed their path. A wind-blown mist cut visibility. Ice caked the rigging. It grew harder and harder for Barents to find a way through the pack. Finally, he told van Heemskerck they must turn back. It was a great disappointment for both men, but their troubles had just started. Sailing westward around the north tip of Novaya Zemlya, they were dismayed to find their retreat blocked by solid ice. The Arctic gave no choice. They must wait until spring.

There, at 77° north latitude, with the ship anchored in a small bay, Barents and van Heemskerck directed the crew in construction of a crude house on shore. Driftwood and planks, taken from above the ship's waterline, formed the siding. Sailcloth served for a roof. The men stocked their house with ship's stores, including the salted beef that had long been standard fare for European sailors. Days shortened rapidly. Winter came with cold winds that moaned through the many cracks of their shelter and made the canvas roof vibrate like a drumskin. But their worst enemy was the salted beef and their ignorance of what it lacked in nourishment. Many of the men broke out with skin sores, particularly on their gums. Ambition and will power left them. Then a man died from that age-old killer of seamen, scurvy, caused as we know now by the lack of vitamins in preserved food. Barents fell ill, perhaps from scurvy, perhaps from a complication of age. Fortunately, when the weather permitted, many of the men hunted the Arctic fox. The pelt made a fine fur cap and the fresh meat provided vitamins enough to keep some of the men healthy.

The men rejoiced at the sun's return, but there was no early thaw of sea ice as hoped. Through May, the ship remained imprisoned. Barents and van Heemskerck decided that the ship's two lifeboats offered the only escape.

Travel in an open boat on the Arctic Ocean, even in springtime, taxes the strength of the healthiest men. Barents was deathly ill at the start of the journey, and died soon after a storm forced the boats to land temporarily on the bleak western shore of Novaya Zemlya. It was June 20, 1597. The rest of the party continued south under van Heemskerck's leadership, and a month after Barents's death, the weary seamen were picked up by two Russian ships and taken to a nearby Dutch vessel, which, by coincidence, was under command of the headstrong Captain Rijp.

Barents had been a dedicated observer, and the charts, sailing instructions, and weather information he compiled were to serve navigators for many years. Moreover, he and van Heemskerck led the first known party of Europeans to return from the Arctic night, a feat that dispelled much unreasoned fear from men's minds. But the gateway to the Northeast Passage, explored though it finally was, did not see another shipping expedition for many years.

The Cossack conquest of Siberia, which began just a few years before Barents's first expedition, eventually revealed the awesome difficulties of the sea passage. The tough Russians pressed farther and farther east, collecting sable and ermine from native hunters. The network of rivers provided easiest travel, and the avid traders with their shallow draft boats earned the title of Freshwater Vikings. They went wherever enough water could be found to float their vessels, but they were forbidden use of the Arctic Ocean. The tsars, who demanded a tenth of all profits, feared the independent Cossacks might try to avoid the levy through smuggling cargoes to Europe by sea. But the sea offered riches in sealskins and walrus ivory. Not every Cossack respected the tsars' prohibition.

In 1648, just fifty-one years after Barents's death, Samyon Ivanovich Deshnev, one of the many agents sent to Siberia to assure collection of the tsar's tenth, sailed out of the mouth of the Kolyma River with a party of six boats. The expedition turned east, skirting the coast. Ice crushed one boat, but no men were lost. Later, when the party tried to land, fierce Chukchis chased the men back to sea. Then a storm struck, scattering the boats.

Deshnev's boat almost sank but finally the tired sailors beached it near the mouth of the Anadyr River. Deshnev knew enough of navigation to realize he had been blown around the eastern limits of the continent and that the land link between Siberia and North America, which some geographers spoke of, did not exist. He dispatched a report to the tsar, but for some reason, either by accident or design, the report was not delivered. Had it been, the next painful ordeal in the search for the Northeast Passage might have been avoided.

Vitus Bering, a Dane serving in the Russian navy, gave thirty-six years and finally his life to exploration. It began in 1725 when Peter the Great sent Bering across Siberia to discover if a ship could sail from the Pacific to the Arctic Ocean.

The tsar, working to build Russia into a nation, recognized the importance of shipping in the development of the Siberian Coast. Bering first traveled by cart and riverboat over four thousand difficult miles to the Sea of Okhotsk. He and his men then built a small boat and crossed to the Kamchatka Peninsula. They toted their supplies over the mountains to the peninsula's eastern shore and built another boat, a brig christened *San Gabriel*. Then, in July of 1728, three years after leaving St. Petersburg, Bering and forty-three men set sail. It was a frustrating voyage. They sailed northeast along the far coast of Asia, found St. Lawrence Island, and then headed into thick fog. Bering took the *San Gabriel* to 67° 18' north latitude, well beyond the Arctic Circle and well through the strait linking Pacific and Arctic waters, a strait that now carries Bering's name, but through it all, fog prevented discovery.

Bering felt sure he had found a strait, but with no chance to define the shore, he could not prove it. When the weary travelers finally returned to St. Petersburg, they received far more criticism than acclaim. Stung by this, Bering determined to go back. Much political wrangling, much debate, and some good sense developed from the suggestion of a second voyage. The government of St. Petersburg finally decided on a massive effort in Siberia, a gathering of all possible scientific information. The project would send scientists to the farthest shores and the highest peaks. It would collect and describe plants and animals. It would take a census of the people and chronicle their history. It would be called the Great Northern Expedition.

Of course, it took time to prepare such a venture, and during that time the long-lost report of Samyon Ivanovich

Deshnev mysteriously came to light. Bering would not have to sail north now. Instead he would sail east to chart the uncertain limits of North America.

Again, he crossed Siberia, and again his shipwrights went to work on the Kamchatka coast. He did not sail into the Pacific until the summer of 1741, and by then the responsibilities of the great undertaking had left him desperately tired. Just the same, he managed to sail his ship to a spectacular Alaskan landfall near what is now called Kayak Island. The snow-capped peaks of the St. Elias Mountains towered above the forested Alaskan coast. Bering and his men had obviously discovered a vast, dramatic, and inviting land, but the leader looked on it with lassitude. He was ill and so were some of the crew. They had sailed too long without fresh food. Bering ordered the ship turned for home. The journey became a desperate race against scurvy. For the ship's doctor, Georg W. Steller, the journey became maddening on two counts.

First, Steller, who had joined the expedition as its botanist, could keep himself healthy by eating the herbs he had collected on Kayak Island, but the crew refused the cure even after a sailor died. Second, Steller was frustrated in his desire to collect specimens on the newly discovered land. While men were filling water casks on Kayak Island, he managed to describe 160 varieties of plants and take notes on many plants and animals. He thus, incidentally, gave his name to the Steller Jay and Steller Sea Lion, but he might have accomplished much more had the anxious Bering not called him back to the ship.

Conditions aboard worsened. Bering fell too ill to command. With poor leadership and worse navigation, the men

mistook the westernmost of the Commander Islands for the
Kamchatka shore. They ran the boat aground and rowed to
the beach before discovering their mistake. They wintered
on the beach in crude shelters of driftwood and stone. Steller
finally persuaded the men to eat his herbs, but it was too
late for some, including Bering. He died and his body was
buried on the island that today carries his name. Those who
survived the winter built a small boat from the timbers and
planks of the ship and sailed safely to Kamchatka, complet-
ing one of the most significant expeditions in Russia's history.

Bering and his men opened an era of fur hunting that gave
Russia domination of the North Pacific for more than a
century and led to Russian ownership of Alaska and Russian
outposts stretching down the coast into California.

Powers in St. Petersburg concluded, after the Great Northern Expedition, which compiled surveys of most of the
Arctic shore line, that the Northeast Passage was not a
feasible trade route. With the wooden sailing ships then
available, this conclusion was quite correct. Not until the
development of steam power and steel ships would serious
thought be given to navigation of the waters explored by
Barents, Deshnev, and Bering.

A Swedish nobleman, veteran of expeditions to Greenland
and the Svalbards, chose the conquest of the Northeast Passage to culminate his career. Baron Nils Adolf Erik Nordenskjöld, with two ships, *Vega* and *Lena,* steamed eastward
early in the summer of 1878. He hoped to reach the Pacific
in one season, but thick fog and ice—particularly around
Cape Chelyuskin, the world's northernmost continental
headland—slowed him. It was late summer by the time he
reached the Lena River delta. There, as planned, the *Lena's*

spare coal was transferred to the *Vega*. Then Nordenskjöld sent *Lena* home. He continued eastward, racing *Vega* against the Arctic winter. Winter won. Ice forced Nordenskjöld to anchor in a sheltered bay little more than one hundred miles from Bering Strait. The bay froze. The ice gripped but did not crush the steel ship. Compared with earlier expeditions, Nordenskjöld and his men had an easy winter. One of the chief difficulties was the heating system, which turned some of the cabins too hot. The men took soundings, sea samples, and weather data. They also made friends with the local residents, the Chukchi. The language barrier at first hampered efforts at trade and conversation, but then, to the surprise of all, one of the young natives began speaking English. He told Nordenskjöld he had picked up the language from English and American whalers, frequent visitors in the Chukchi Sea.

Ice held the *Vega* until a sudden break-up in July of 1879. Steam was raised at once, and the ship soon nosed eastward through a calm sea whose surface was disturbed only by a few curious walruses who raised their tusks and whiskered faces to watch *Vega* pass.

Nordenskjöld's historic voyage was financed in part by a Russian shipowner. This was certainly appropriate. Opening of the passage brightened Russia's economic future, but it took many more years to develop the route, and there were some serious mistakes. In 1933, for instance, the Soviets tried to send a cargo ship *Chelyuskin* through the route without adequate support from icebreakers. Ice trapped and crushed her in the Chukchi Sea, and only by a daring air rescue were her people saved.

Today, the Soviets have the largest, best-equipped fleet of

icebreakers in the world. These stout boats, including the giant, 435-foot, atomic-powered *Lenin,* keep the 6,000-mile Northeast Passage open three months each summer, allowing annual movement of an average 2 million tons of cargo. Though not a significant route between Europe and the Orient, as once imagined, the passage links Siberia with world markets.

4

Northwest and the Pole

WHILE VICTORY OVER the Northeast Passage came after considerable patience, after adequate ships had been developed, the struggle for the Northwest Passage was marked by costly impatience, heroics, and tragedy. It began in 1576 when Sir Martin Frobisher, who was later to fight with Drake against the Spanish Armada, sailed into the sea between Greenland and Baffin Island and searched for a way west. No one conquered the passage until early in this century when Roald Amundsen and six Norwegian countrymen worked a fishing smack from the Atlantic to the Pacific in a three-year voyage.

Actually, search for a practical Northwest Passage continues today.

Frobisher made three voyages into a dead-end bay which now bears his name. His interest in a trade route was diverted by what he thought was gold ore. He might have continued hauling shiploads of this stuff to England until the end of his days had chemists not discovered it to be worthless pyrite or fool's gold. Frobisher turned elsewhere for adventure. But other English explorers soon picked up where he left off. John Davis and William Baffin sailed the waters earlier coursed by Erik the Red. They produced serviceable charts, making it much easier for those who followed. The English navigator Henry Hudson, whose work for the Dutch included the discovery of the Hudson River, was commissioned by England in 1609 to find the Northwest Passage. He found instead the strait and huge inland sea which both bear his name. Hudson, his young son, and seven sick crewmen were cast adrift in a small boat by a crew who mutinied against further cruising of the inland sea. Hudson died thinking he had found the passage west. What he had found prompted formation of the Hudson's Bay Company, an enterprise that would exploit and dominate the Canadian north for more than two hundred years.

Long after Spain and Portugal lost control of the southern routes to the Orient, the Northwest Passage remained a goal in the minds of men, particularly Englishmen. In 1819, British naval lieutenant William Edward Parry almost won through. With two square riggers, *Hecla* and *Gripper,* he sailed from Baffin Bay due west through Lancaster Sound, Barrow Strait, and on into Viscount Melville Sound where

heavy ice forced him to winter and later turn back. By passing 110° west longitude, Parry and his man divided a
£5,000 award from the British government. Their record
westing was to stand for almost a century.

In 1845, an experienced Arctic explorer, 59-year-old Sir
John Franklin, decided to try for the passage. His attempt
ended in one of the most publicized tragedies of the last
century. With two barks, *Erebus* and *Terror,* Franklin entered Lancaster Sound, but instead of following Parry's
track, he turned south into Peel Strait. He hoped to find
passage along the shore of the Canadian mainland, a shore
he knew well from previous land expeditions, but he did
not reckon on the ice northwest of King William Island. It
trapped both ships in a grip of death. The men waited, hoping for release. Stores diminished. Seamen began to die.
Franklin died in June of 1847. The following spring, survivors of the expedition started walking south over the ice.
Most were weak and near starvation, but a few managed to
reach the Canadian mainland near the mouth of Back River.
They hoped to find good hunting and fishing there, but they
lacked the native skill and patience. Here the last of an
original party of 129 men died.

For ten years, fate of the expedition remained unknown
and many search parties ranged the scattered islands and
waterways of the Arctic Archipelago. Rewards were posted.
Searches were financed by both the United States and
England. There was private financing as well. Lady Jane
Franklin exhausted her wealth in sending men to find her
husband. In 1855, a party of Eskimos on Boothia Peninsula
told a searcher of forty starving white men who had marched

south several summers back. Then in 1857 a brief note was found in a rock pile on King William Island telling of Franklin's death and the march south.

The searches for Franklin, while they took their own toll of men and wealth, all but filled in the blanks in the map of the far north. Foundation for final assault on the passage was complete. English, Canadian, and United States explorers did the groundwork, but it was Amundsen, whom men called the last of the Vikings, who first sailed the Northwest Passage.

The Norwegian, who began preparing himself for exploration early in life, carefully converted *Gjoa,* a 72-foot fishing smack for the assault. He selected his small crew with equal care, but lack of money almost defeated his ambition. When he finally sailed in 1903, he left harbor secretly in the middle of a stormy night to avoid court action by an angry creditor.

Amundsen followed Franklin's route with one important variation. Instead of trying to force the ice northwest of King William Island, he sailed the *Gjoa* around the shoal channel to the southeast. The smack scraped her keel on jagged rocks and once went so hard aground that the men had to jettison cargo to lighten her. Finally she made the shelter of Peterson Bay. Here the Norwegians set up camp ashore. They stayed two winters, gathering detailed magnetic and weather information. From the base camp, called Gjoahaven, Amundsen led a sledge party to the Boothia Peninsula and located the magnetic pole just a few miles from the spot where Sir James Clark Ross had found it in 1831. Another dog sledge party went westward and returned with detailed charts of the southern coast of Victoria Island.

In addition to these accomplishments, the men established excellent relations with Eskimos, and during the second year, one hundred Eskimo families camped at Gjoahaven. In the summer of 1905, after sad farewells, the men pulled up anchor and sailed from the sheltered bay toward the west. Amundsen did not complete the journey that season as hoped. Ice forced another winter anchorage, this one off the Yukon shore in company with American whalers. There one of his men died from an undiagnosed intestinal ailment, and a young Eskimo boy who had sailed with them from Gjoahaven drowned while hunting ducks. These tragedies tempered the victory, but when Amundsen and his men finally sailed into San Francisco they were welcomed as heroes. The expedition produced much scientific data. Amundsen's accounts of the native ways[8] still provide informative reading, but the voyage itself showed that the route of the *Gjoa* was too shallow to ever serve as passage for cargo vessels.

Both United States and Canadian icebreakers have since forced the direct passage that Parry almost achieved a century and a half ago. The first cargo vessel ever to attempt this route sailed north in 1969. She was the tanker *Manhattan,* a giant, 1,005-foot ship built, equipped, and manned at a cost of $43 million, put up mostly by Humble Oil and Refining Company. The company was gambling on surface shipping as the best way to transport the recently discovered oil of Alaska's North Slope to the world markets. Though assisted by icebreakers, pack ice forced the big ship to turn south through Prince of Wales Strait. This was not a real problem. *Manhattan* made it unscathed to Alaska's Prudhoe

Bay. Matter-of-fact account books showed the real problem. Transporting oil by surface ship through Arctic waters was simply too costly.

But oilmen and shippers have not given up. They are thinking now of passage under the ice by giant atomic-powered submarines. Such vessels would make the north-west trade route a reality.

The effort to reach the North Pole also began with trade as the goal. England's Henry VIII sent two ships north in 1527 to find the Orient. The logic was that the earth, which almost everyone finally agreed really was round, would provide a pathway to the East across its top just as readily as east or west. Henry's ships, however, never returned. Both were lost in a violent storm near Greenland. The motivation soon switched from trade to curiosity. In addition, the pole became a symbolic goal, a test of manliness, heroics, stamina, and courage.

For years, the rumor held that the North Pole lay on an island or a continent. In 1578 Gerardus Mercator published an imaginative map showing a circular continent with four rivers flowing from the pole to the sea like evenly spaced spokes of a wheel. In 1607, Hudson, who would die two years later in the New World, sailed beyond the Svalbards to 80° 23′ north latitude, farther than any ship had yet gone. He saw no land. Hudson's record stood until 1772 when English navigator C. J. Phipps extended man's northern horizon by another twenty-five miles. Phipps found no land. In 1827, Parry, of Northwest Passage fame, became the first to try sledging north over the ice. He reached 82° 48′ north lati-tude, a new record, before open water stopped him. If land lay to the north, Parry reported, it was hardly the continent that Mercator had suggested.

During the search for Franklin, Elisha Kent Kane, an American explorer and writer, poked into the narrow waters between Greenland and Ellesmere Island. Smith Sound, Kane Basin, and Kennedy and Robeson channels became known collectively as the American Passage.

In 1871, American naval officer Charles Francis Hall made use of this passage to sail to 82° 11′ north latitude, closer than any ship had yet come to the pole. Five years later, the English explorer Lt. (later Sir) Albert Hastings Markham sledged to a new record—83° 20′ north latitude.

Looking to the other side of the Arctic, another American naval officer, George Washington De Long, proposed to reach the pole on a warm current that he believed flowed north from the Pacific through Bering Strait. He sailed in 1879. Instead of finding open water, as hoped, the De Long party found ice that trapped and eventually crushed the ship. The horrible struggle across ice and over water by open boat to search for aid in sparsely settled Siberia took a cruel toll. More than half the party, including De Long, died from exhaustion and starvation. But the current De Long sought did seem to flow under the ice, carrying the pack slowly with it. Three years after the tragedy, a provision list, a seaman's cap, and other relics from the De Long ship washed ashore on the coast of Greenland.

This prompted great debate among Arctic scholars. Some thought the relics could be nothing but the products of some prankster, but a Norwegian explorer and professor was fascinated. He knew already that Siberian larch, which could only come from the north-flowing rivers of Asia, drifted to Greenland's shore. Fridtjof Nansen felt sure an east-west polar current existed. He planned to prove it.

What Nansen proposed shocked fellow scientists. He would sail deliberately into the ice, let his ship be entrapped, and then drift with the pack across the top of the world. Many friends and scholars predicted sure death, but Nansen planned well. His ship, *Fram,* was designed with sharply sloped rather than vertical sides. The lateral ice pressure would lift rather than crush the vessel.

With eleven other countrymen, Nansen set sail in the summer of 1893. The ice encircled *Fram* north of the New Siberia Islands, and just as Nansen predicted, the first pressure lifted her comfortably out of danger. But the drift did not carry the ship as far north as Nansen had hoped. It soon became clear that their track would not cross the North Pole.

Nansen had always insisted that the achievement of the pole had little significance in scientific inquiry. By measuring water depths and temperatures, ice thickness, wind velocity, air pressure, and temperature, the expedition could produce much valuable information on the Arctic without reaching the pole. Yet as the months passed, as the ship drifted closer, the historic goal beckoned. On March 14, 1895, Nansen and crewman Hjalmar Johansen left the shelter of the *Fram* and made a dash toward the North Pole by dog sledge.

Pressure ridges turned travel into hard labor. Cargo, sledges, and dogs had to be man-handled over wall after wall of jumbled ice blocks. Some of these barriers rose twenty feet high. In addition, a current worked against the sledgers. They could struggle all day but gain just a few miles over the current. On April 9, they reluctantly turned away. Nansen and Johansen had traveled to 86° 16.3′ north latitude, just

224 nautical miles from the North Pole. No man had come so close.[9]

The two men never entertained the hope of connecting with the *Fram*. Their plan was to sledge to Franz Josef Land or the Svalbards and find a ship, perhaps a sealer, that could take them home. The journey took far longer than expected. Slush ice and open water slowed and diverted them. They had brought rations for a hundred days and planned to kill the dogs gradually as the loads lightened. Dog flesh would be fed the surviving dogs. The dog killing, much to the men's regret, began soon after turning south. When just a few dogs remained, one of them saved Johansen's life during a polar bear's sudden attack. The bear knocked Johansen down and was about to bite him when a dog drew the beast off. It gave Nansen time to get his rifle and kill the bear.

Finally, at the edge of the ice, it was time to take to the two kayaks that had been lashed atop the sledges. Tearfully, the men killed the last two dogs. These survivors had become close companions in a lonely world.

In late August, five months after leaving *Fram,* the men landed on Jackson Island, a western outpost of Franz Josef Land. They built a winter shelter of rock, driftwood, and skins and busily laid in a supply of seal meat and blubber. Ice surrounded the island. Without dogs, they knew it would be a long time before they could travel again. Patiently they waited through the long night. Winds whistled around their shelter almost constantly, but there were also some moments of calm when they could stand outside, look up at the brilliant aurora, and marvel.

On May 19, 1896, with the ice in retreat, Nansen and

Johansen sailed from the island, continuing the journey south. After a few weeks, while camped on Cape Flora, the men heard a dog barking. Nansen investigated. He soon found himself shaking hands with a smiling man dressed in rubber boots, checked suit, and fur cap. It was Frederick Jackson of England's Jackson-Harmsworth Expedition. He had come out from his camp with his dog for a morning stroll. Other than Johansen, this was the first human Nansen had gazed upon in fourteen months.

The Englishmen received the two Norwegians warmly, and when the expedition's support ship arrived, Nansen and Johansen were delivered home to a triumphant welcome. That was August 13, 1896. The very next day, *Fram* returned. She had cleared the ice west of Spitsbergen after drifting to 85° 57′ north latitude.

The *Fram* venture, both bold and scientifically productive, just about silenced talk of land at the pole. Nansen's soundings, showing depths of nearly two miles, made chances of any substantial land masses highly unlikely. Temperature readings of the depths showed a warm layer of water sandwiched between upper and lower cold layers. Nansen recognized this warm layer as the last of the north-flowing Atlantic currents. Nansen's experience also demonstrated that the best time for Arctic sledging was winter and early spring. Only then could a man cover good distance without interruption by open water.

During Nansen's historic venture, Robert Edwin Peary, an engineering officer in the United States Navy, was gaining Arctic knowledge in surveying the north of Greenland. A single ambition drove this tall, lean officer. He wanted to lead the first party to the North Pole. In an 1899 expedition to

Ellesmere Island, frostbite took all but the little toes of each foot, but the following year Peary made his first attempt at the pole. His second came in 1902, his third in 1906. He used platoons of sledges to break trail and relay supplies. He also used Eskimo drivers and he and the other Americans in his parties wore Eskimo clothing, spoke Eskimo, learned to make snow igloos, and learned to respect Eskimo knowledge of weather and ice. But time and again, Peary failed to reach his goal. If open water or rough ice did not turn him back, shortage of supplies did. He prepared another assault in 1908. He was fifty-two years old. He knew it would be his last.

It was a rough beginning. Temperature at the start stood at —50° F. Sledges broke in bumping over pressure ice. Kerosene for the stoves leaked from the cans, and Peary had to send back one platoon to fetch more. Then open water forced a halt. Some of the Eskimos, fearing that *Tornarsuk,* the devil of the north, was against them, threatened to turn back. But somehow, all these difficulties were overcome, and the sledges pressed on as soon as the open lead closed. Peary began sending home tired men and dogs. Tragedy hit the expedition when Ross Marvin, a young engineering professor, made the error of scouting ahead of his platoon on the return to base camp. He fell through slush ice and drowned.

Peary, who did not learn of Marvin's death until his own return, pressed on, continuing to send back support platoons. Finally, he and his Negro aide, Matthew Henson, with four Eskimos, were all that remained of an original force of twenty-three men. They enjoyed surprisingly good sledging, clear weather, and mile after mile of smooth ice. On April 9, 1909, the six men reached the North Pole.

Peary's victory showed that the pole stood in the heart of a frozen sea. There was no land. The exploit also showed what courage, determination, and stamina could accomplish, but the scientific yield was not great. And soon after Peary returned to the United States, Dr. Frederick Cook announced that he and two Eskimos had sledged to the pole the previous winter. Cook, a member of one of Peary's earlier expeditions, had also served with distinction on a nearly disastrous Belgian venture to the Antarctic. His conflicting claim touched off a public controversy that raged through America for months. It eventually moved the United States Congress to action. The politicians voted to recognize Peary's as the just claim. Cook, later convicted of mail fraud, was generally discredited. But for years afterward the subject prompted argument.

5

Polar Flight

ADVANCE IN POLAR flight paralleled development of the aircraft. The daring pilots who winged north often had dual motives. They wanted to expand the horizon of discovery and they also sought to justify their faith in flight.

In 1897, Swedish university professor Salomon August Andrée and two countrymen tried to reach the North Pole by balloon, but cold mists sheathed their craft with ice, weighing it lower and lower. It crashed on the frozen sea just a few days after taking off from Danes Island in the Svalbards. The men were 480 miles short of the pole. With terrible difficulty, the balloonists made their way south to uninhabited White Island in the Svalbards. Their camp and their bodies were found there thirty-three years later. Cause of death long remained a mystery, but recent tests of a bearskin found in the camp put the blame strongly on trichinosis in the bear's flesh.

In 1914, during a futile search for a sledge party, a Lieutenant Nagurskiy of Russia made five flights in a small seaplane from Novaya Zemlya and became the first man in history to pilot a heavier-than-air craft in the Arctic. Following World War I and the rapid technical advances it prompted, pilots became more venturesome, governments far more interested. In 1920, a United States Army Air Service flight of four war planes from New York to Nome, Alaska, and back, pointed to the need for more reliable weather forecasting and more accurate maps.

Amundsen, with conquest of the South Pole as well as the Northwest Passage behind him, took great interest in flying as a means of exploration. In 1925, with two huge Dornier Wal flying boats, he led an expedition from Spitsbergen north. Big as they were, the planes lacked the range to reach the pole and return, but Amundsen hoped to find open water, land, transfer gasoline and men from one machine to the other, and continue in a single craft. The notion was foolhardy. The planes did land, not in open water but in slush ice many miles short of the pole. The men were able to transfer very little fuel. The plane could not take off from the slush. For days, Amundsen and his crew hauled and packed ice for a runway. Amundsen estimated later that they moved five hundred tons of ice. Then with the help of a rare spring freeze that hardened the runway, the lumbering craft, using every last foot of level space, managed to climb free. The men reached Spitsbergen exhausted but unharmed twenty-six days after their unsuccessful venture began.

The first successful flight to the pole was made in 1926 by Americans Floyd Bennett and Richard E. Byrd. They used a Fokker trimotor equipped with ski landing gear. Amundsen's experience had shown the limitations of float planes in the far north. Bennett and Byrd had their greatest difficulty in taking off from their snow-packed runway at King's Bay, Spitsbergen. Several times, the plane plowed into snowbanks at the end of the field, but finally after emergency sledging gear and food were taken off the fuel-heavy plane, and after the enthusiastic ground crew lengthened the runway, the Fokker rose in the sky and turned north.

In addition to violent weather, Arctic flying posed another serious problem. Close to the magnetic pole, the magnetic compass became unreliable, and for the pioneers in flight, working out sextant shots of stars or the sun often took too much time. When Byrd and Bennett made their flight, tables short-cutting the navigation formulae had just been worked out. They carried these, but the greatest aid was the sun compass. Both men had tested this the previous year while on an aerial survey in Greenland. It used the sundial principle. While a sundial tells time when oriented with the direction, the sun compass tells direction to the navigator who knows the time. Early in their flight, Byrd took many sextant shots and scanned the ice surface again and again to check wind speed and drift. Later, as his confidence grew, he relied more on the sun compass.

Byrd's calculations showed that at 9:02 A.M. Greenwich time, May 9, 1926, they were over the pole. They looked down upon an endless expanse of ice. Bennett banked the plane in a wide circle, taking them around the world in a matter of minutes. Byrd took sights to confirm the goal. Then they headed south.

The flight from Spitsbergen to the pole and back, 1,600 miles, took fifteen and a half hours. First to greet the fliers on their return was Amundsen. After his flying boat experience, the energetic Norwegian had decided to fly to the pole in the Italian built dirigible *Norge*. Now that Byrd and Bennett had beaten him, Amundsen changed his plans. When the *Norge,* with her designer Umberto Nobile at the controls, rose from Spitsbergen two days after Byrd's flight, her goal was Nome, Alaska, and her route would make her the first aircraft to cross the Arctic Ocean. Ice caked on her propellers and big chunks of it slammed against the skin of the ship again and again. Fog and headwinds slowed her, but *Norge* completed the voyage in seventy hours and forty minutes, landing at Teller just seventy miles short of Nome.

Unfortunately, Amundsen and Nobile argued violently after the flight over publication rights on the venture. Amundsen considered the Italian no more than his hired pilot.[10] Nobile, however, took great national pride in both the ship and its Italian crewmen. The public dispute was bitter, doing discredit to both men, but when Nobile crashed on the ice in 1928 during a polar flight in *Norge's* sister ship, Amundsen forgot their differences at once and was among the first to volunteer in the search for Nobile and his companions. The men were eventually found, but the plane carrying Amundsen to the search area crashed in the sea with no survivors.

One of Amundsen's last public statements before his death

was made in praise of a persistent Australian explorer, George Hubert (later Sir Hubert) Wilkins. Wilkins, with American Carl Ben Eielson at the controls, had just flown a single-engine, Lockheed Vega from Point Barrow, Alaska, to Green Harbor, Spitsbergen, 2,200 miles over the ice to the north of the Arctic Archipelago and Greenland. The Vega reached Spitsbergen during a blinding blizzard, and only by the greatest luck and skill did Eielson manage to put the ship down on a desolate island. Their flight had taken twenty hours and twenty minutes. The storm grounded them for four days, but finally they managed to get aloft with just enough gas for the short hop to the Norwegian weather station at Green Harbor. For the two men, the successful flight culminated three frustrating years in the Arctic. Expensive planes had crashed during test flights, weather often prevented transport of supplies to Point Barrow, and Wilkins's original backers, a group of Detroit businessmen, eventually cut all support. Once, Wilkins and Eielson crash-landed on the ice north of Point Barrow. It took thirty-three days to walk back to shore. Despite all these setbacks, Wilkins was convinced that flight was the key to Arctic travel. He stuck with that conviction until he proved it. The only major limit remaining was range of the aircraft.

In 1937, Russia startled the aviation world by sending a single-engine aircraft non-stop from Moscow to a field near Portland, Oregon, a 5,507-mile flight across the North Pole. Called the ANT-25, the plane had a single wing, wide and long for superb lifting power. Her three-bladed propeller for more pull and her retractable landing gear for streamlining were innovations. Until its flight, observers outside Russia thought the country had nothing that could stay aloft more than six hours. In its historic flight, the ANT-25 was in the air sixty hours and thirty minutes.

Though the Russian plane vastly extended the range of flight, it had serious limitations for the Arctic skies. Her pilots, Valery Chkalov and George Baidukov, and her radioman, M. Beliakov, suffered from cold in the poorly heated cabin. Oxygen supply was severely limited, but most serious of all was icing. Alcohol jets were supposed to keep ice off the propeller and wings, but the supply of alcohol was quickly expended. The pilots repeatedly had to change altitude to get out of icing zones. When forced high, the men suffered from drowsiness and slow reactions in the thin air. Cold inside the ship nearly brought disaster when the radiator of the water-cooled motor boiled over. Because of the cold, water in a reserve radiator tank had frozen. Luckily there was some unfrozen drinking water which served to prime the pump and move enough from the reserve tank to the radiator to bring the engine temperature back to a safe level.

There was another deficiency. Radioman Beliakov managed to reach an Alaskan weather station, but he could not get the forecast. No one on the ground spoke Russian and no one in the plane spoke English.

World War II forced all major nations to concentrate on military aircraft. Though the technical advances were all aimed at making a better weapon, there were many improvements that had general application to safety and efficiency of the airplane. The war also produced well-trained and experienced airmen. In the north, the United States war against the Japanese on the Aleutian Islands was largely an air war. Those who survived the blinding, wind-driven fogs, the sub-

zero temperatures and difficulties of navigation and communication could handle the worst the Arctic offered.

By the time the war ended, the United States had supreme
confidence in her planes and her men. Flight of the *Pacusan
Dreamboat,* a B-29 superfortress, demonstrated that confidence. The big bomber flew non-stop from Hawaii over the
pole to Cairo, Egypt, 9,422 miles in thirty-nine hours and
thirty-five minutes. The new distance record heralded the
return of peace and reopened the assault on Arctic skies.

But the United States Arctic interests were shaped by the
Cold War. With Russia commanding so much of the Arctic's
shore, flight either by rockets or planes brought military
threat. At great expense, the United States Air Force began
building bases across the American shores of the Arctic from
Alaska to Greenland. Peaceful use of the Arctic skies was
neglected.

Thus, in 1954, airline interests in Norway, Sweden, and
Denmark, joined as the Scandinavian Airline System, became
the first to launch commercial flights by the polar route.
SAS used an American-built plane for its first passenger and
cargo flights, the Douglas DC6b, and it relied on United
States military bases for fuel stops and weather reports.

Today, commercial lines from many nations use the polar
route with flights from terminals in Northern Europe,
America's West Coast, and Japan. The route, shorter than
conventional spans of the Atlantic or Pacific oceans, can be
flown non-stop by modern jets and leave range to spare at
the end of the flights should rerouting be necessary. By flying
high, the planes avoid storms, and if a liner ever should be
forced down, its crew and passengers would have a far better
chance for survival on ice than in the open sea.

An average of five jetliners a day use the polar route. Passengers who look down on the Arctic ice might well marvel at the way the air age and technology have changed the world. A passenger in a comfortable chair can read a book while soft music plays, and below lies an arena of struggle, a goal that drew upon the energies, the stamina, and the will power of man through 2,300 years. No region of the world contrasts the old and the new more than the Arctic.

6

Sea Hunt

Explorers were not the only early mariners to pass beyond the Arctic Circle. Whalers and sealers sailed in the wake of discovery, and sometimes, as Nordenskjöld found to his surprise, these bold sea hunters entered uncharted waters well ahead of exploration.

Over the years, whalers and sealers built a romantic history, peopled with daring heroes, individualists following the lure of wealth and adventure. Extremes of good and evil have marked whaling and sealing through the centuries. Few of man's ventures have tested courage so severely. Few have caused such merciless slaughter.

Commercial whaling waxed so intense that today whalers of many nations find it unprofitable. There simply are not enough whales left.

Stone-Age man hunted seals from Alaska's Cape Krusenstern at least five thousand years ago. Whalers camped there four thousand years ago. From stone knives and lance points and ivory toggles for harpoons, Giddings and fellow archaeologists surmised that the Old Whalers, as he called them, hunted in much the same manner as the Eskimos who followed.

Early observers of Eskimo whaling describe how eight men would put out in an umiak as soon as beach watchers saw the steam-white exhalations or blows of passing whales. The umiak was a high-sided open boat of skins stretched on a light frame. At the bow stood the harpooner, at the stern the helmsman. The other six men paddled furiously, sending the light boat speeding toward the whales. The helmsman would not call a halt to the paddling until the whale's flank was almost under the bow. Then the harpooner struck. The point of his harpoon, an ivory or bone toggle, turned sideways and stuck fast under the skin as soon as the harpooner's line pulled tight. The wound did little harm to the whale, but air-filled skin bladders tied to the harpoon line created a drag that tired the whale in its effort to escape. The bladders also marked the whale's progress so hunters could follow. Eventually the whale tired enough so the umiak could be brought close enough for the men to use their lances. They drove the flint-tipped weapons either into vital nerves at the base of the whale's brain or through its lungs. If the whale did not smash the fragile boat or break free, the hunters towed the huge beast back to shore in slow triumph. Women waited with stone knives to cut the blubber and carve the meat.

The Eskimos used a similar toggle and air-bladder system to take walruses. Many times, the whales or the walruses broke free, maybe to survive, maybe to die of wounds and wash ashore far from the hunt. This prompted the only known instance of Eskimo writing. The hunter scratched a distinctive mark on his harpoon so he could claim his animals even if they beached far from his home.

Natives of the Aleutian Islands once hunted with poisoned harpoons, trusting that the whale, once it died, might drift ashore nearby.

Eskimos today still hunt whales, but large varieties are seldom seen. The common quarry is the beluga or white whale, a ten-footer prized for its skin and blubber which is cut into strips for *muktuk*. The natives chew this like taffy sticks.

Though the Old Whalers of Cape Krusenstern may have taught their neighbors how to hunt whales, they left little else for Arctic posterity. Their notched spear and lance points link them more closely to the American Indian. The points also suggest a European rather than Asian origin.

Native whale hunters never endangered a species. The whales may have grown cautious about approaching certain shores, but most of their vast, watery world held no threat. They continued to roam a domain they had ruled for millions of years, the largest animals ever known, cruising toward a fateful encounter with modern man.

Scientists tell us that whales evolved from creatures that once walked on land. Of course, in this early stage of evolution, they had a different form, not so ponderous, and equipped with four legs. A few vestigial bones beneath the whale's skin are all that remain of the hind legs.

There are two classes of whales: those with teeth, such as the sperm whale and killer whale; and those with baleen or whalebone—fibrous slats that hang from the roof of the whale's mouth and serve as sieves in collecting food from the sea. Many kinds of baleen whales are ponderously slow swimmers, making them relatively easy prey for man.

The first victim was *Balaena Biscayensis* or the Basque whale which passed close to the coast of Spain and Portugal and cruised into the Bay of Biscay. Portuguese and Basque fishermen first learned to value whale oil for lamps from the few animals that were beached by storms or killer whales. By the twelfth century, fishermen began rowing from shore in small boats to harpoon the whales. The Basques grew particularly skillful, and as demand for whale oil increased, they intensified the hunt.

Whale meat, while perhaps not as tasty as beef or lamb, was nourishing enough. Actually, whale tongue became a prized delicacy. The devout Basques often gave the tongue to monks of nearby monasteries. Whalebone, or baleen, also found a market, one of its first uses being as a stiffener to hold the plume of a knight's helmet proudly aloft.

The Basques built towers for lookouts who beat drums or rang bells the moment they saw a whale. Whalers then rushed for their boats. Except for the use of iron-pointed harpoons and lances, the hunt differed little from the Eskimo method. The whale was towed ashore, where its blubber was rendered into oil in big tubs over open fires. Basque whaling boomed. Kings demanded a royalty, but that reduced profits only slightly. There was only one limitation to the industry

—the whales themselves. Fewer and fewer swam near the shore. The Basques changed tactics. They began hunting from ships. These were cramped square riggers called *rafiots*. Lookouts, instead of standing atop a shore tower, searched from the masthead, but when whales were sighted, similar small boats were launched from ship, and the chase was pressed in the same manner as before. Captured whales were hauled back to the ship and butchered alongside. Ship's tackle hoisted aboard the strips of blubber, meat, and bone as men cut up the carcass. A *rafiot,* returning after a long voyage, brought with it the stench of rancid blubber. For those living aboard, the smell must have been almost stifling. But the Basques ranged farther from home as the whale population diminished. The hunt led to the Arctic. By 1520, Basque *rafiots* cruised the waters between Greenland and Baffin Island.

The long voyages forced another change: rending blubber at sea. A Basque skipper named Sopite, sailing out of St. Jean de Luz, is said to have been the first to build a brick hearth on the deck of his ship, render the blubber in try pots, and store his oil in barrels. The process not only increased storage capacity on board but also improved the smell of the ship.

By the time of this development, however, Basque whalers had company. Scottish, English, French, and Dutch ships had joined the hunt late in the fifteenth century. At first these ships carried Basques to handle the difficult parts of the venture, but the Basque had many eager pupils. It did not take long for the pupils to replace their teachers, and the pupils were generally ungrateful. Basque *rafiots* sometimes fled from the old whaling grounds with cannon fire from an English or Dutch ship booming after them. By the end of the sixteenth century, Basques no longer dominated the industry they had developed. The Basque methods, however, continued almost into this century.

The last of Basque whales vanished about the same time as the Basques stopped whaling. Whalers next sought the right whale. It grew to fifty or sixty feet, a little smaller than the Basque whale, but its oil was just as good and it too was a slow swimmer, just as easily taken. Its baleen, up to seven feet long, was more valuable than the shorter bone of the Basque whale, and baleen had found many more uses. Corset stays, buggy whips, fishing rods, and umbrella spokes were made from whalebone, and the price for good whalebone eventually rose to five dollars per pound. The right whale had just one disadvantage: its summer migration took it far north, so that whalers had to sail to the very edge of the ice.

The Dutch solved the problem by establishing a seasonal base on Spitsbergen, a whaling factory employing thousands of men where ships could bring their whales to be rendered. Summertown, Blubbertown, and Smeeringburg were some of the names for this station. It continued throughout the eighteenth century, but ceased to exist when the whales of the region gave out.

To the west, good whaling in Davis Strait and Baffin Bay lasted longer. One whaling captain counted 355 whalers in these waters in 1722. It was dangerous territory. More than five hundred whaling ships have been lost to ice in the Davis Strait and Baffin Bay region. While whaling was hard on men and ships, it was much harder on the whale.

When the right whale became scarce, whalers took the bowhead. This was slightly larger than the right whale and it had much more valuable baleen, ten to twelve feet long in the adult whales. But no species could be found that could withstand the slaughter. The herds diminished. Today, the Basque whale is extinct and the bowhead is so rare that only Eskimos are allowed to take a limited number. Under controls, the right whale has recovered enough for some whaling, but by past standards, the baleen whale industry of the North Atlantic is dead. The decline actually began late in the eighteenth century. American whalers were among the first to recognize the change.

On his voyage to the New World, Captain John Smith found so many whales off the American coast that he delayed landing to pursue them. New Englanders, with rocky soil and poor farms, took to the sea for their livelihood, a sea that then swarmed with summer herds of whales. The hunting method was much like that developed by Basques years earlier with boats putting out from shore and hauling captured whales back to the beach for rendering. Seamen of New Bedford and Nantucket Island became experts, but as in the past, the whales grew scarce. Nantucket whalers began sailing from shore in small sloops with capacity for the blubber from a single whale. At home after a successful voyage, the sloops were beached broadside and the blubber was hauled off to tryworks. Later, bigger ships sailed after whales and, by 1715, the Nantucket whalers carried the tryworks on deck. British whalers found that by basing their fleets in the colonies, the ships could reach untouched whaling grounds from Newfoundland to Brazil. Profits increased, the industry grew. Then the Revolutionary War brought disaster.

At the start of the war, the Royal Navy seized every American ship it could find. Nantucket alone lost 134 whalers. The war also meant the withdrawal of British investment, and when the fighting ended, the British whaling fleet had moved to Halifax, Nova Scotia. Some New Englanders worked out of Halifax on British ships during the post-war years, but most became dissatisfied and went home where a new fleet was building. Soon American whaling began to flourish once more. Without British restrictions and taxes the potential seemed to have no limit. But, of course, nature had a limit in the supply of whales.

In 1790, harvest from old whaling grounds was falling rapidly when the British whaler *Emilia* returned from a cruise west of Cape Horn. She was the first European whaler to hunt in the Pacific, and she brought home a full cargo of sperm oil. American skippers lost no time following the *Emilia*'s lead. *Beaver* out of Nantucket with Paul Worth as captain sailed into the Pacific in search of sperm whales in 1791. Worth filled his barrels after just a few months of cruising. This was good hunting.

True, the sperm whale lacked the valuable baleen, but its oil commanded top price, and the wax-like spermaceti, found in the head, was valued by candle makers. Sometimes, if a ship was lucky, ambergris might be found in a sperm whale's intestine. This jelly-like secretion could be sold at twenty-five dollars an ounce to perfume makers. Sperm whales were more dangerous than baleens, but there were men enough to face the challenge, men willing to roam the oceans of the world on cruises that lasted three, four, and sometimes five years. For a time, British and American whalers vied for supremacy in the sperm-oil trade. The War of 1812 settled the competition. While many American whalers were seized at the start of the war, the United States frigate *Essex,* cruising the Pacific, captured, sank, or destroyed scores of British ships and the British industry never regained its former strength.

With the treaty of 1814, American whaling took on new life. No longer did ship owners and seamen fear British impressment. Businessmen looked upon whaling as a sound investment. New whaling grounds were discovered. In 1835, the *Ganges* out of Nantucket entered the North Pacific and sighted thousands of whales. In 1843, the New Bedford vessels, *Hercules* and *Janus,* took bowhead whales off the coast of the Kamchatka Peninsula. Five years later, the Yankee whaler *Superior* worked through Bering Strait into the Chukchi Sea to take bowheads.

It was a great seafaring era for America, an exciting era when the masthead call of "She blows! She blows! Thar she blows!" would bring spirited men running to the deck and dashing for the boats. The average ship would launch three, sometimes four, whaleboats. These were small—thirty feet long and six feet wide—but they were designed perfectly for the task. They carried a crew of six. Five men pulled oars while an officer stood at the helm. The bow oarsman was also harpooner, but he rowed with the rest until the officer steered the boat within range. Then the harpooner shipped his oar, snatched up his harpoon, and turned to face the whale. If the sight of the monster's flank so close before him made him nervous, he had little time to think about it for the harpoon had to be driven home at once. The harpooner thrust the double-barbed point of his weapon with all his strength. Immediately, the helmsman ordered the rowers to back the boat. No one could tell what the whale would do. It might sound, running the line from the tub and through the bow chocks so fast that the hemp smoked. Or the whale might try to flee on the surface carrying the boat after it in a crazy, spray-dashing race that sailors called a Nantucket sleigh ride. Sometimes an angry whale might turn on a boat. Its flukes could smash the frail craft to splinters with one blow. There were times when the sperm whale did not limit its wrath to the small boats. Records tell of three stout whale ships rammed and sunk by whales.

Whales were not the only danger. Despite the improved medical knowledge of the last century, men still died of scurvy. Some ships returned to home ports with half of their original crew. To the shame of ship owners and masters the tradition of salt beef and dried biscuit held through most of America's whaling era. There were other needless losses. Logs of ships captured by ice in the Arctic tell of long, dreary winters when discipline waned and morale disintegrated. Men would wander aimlessly from the ships, never to return.

Storms and mutiny also took toll of men and ships, but in the face of it all new whaling ventures were mounted and manned again and again. There was money to be made in whaling. Profits of each successful voyage, after the ship owner's share, were divided among the crew according to rank. The share, or lay as it was called, could be substantial. The record of the New Bedford whaler *Milton,* returning from a voyage in 1836 showed $5,882 for the captain and $4,545 for the first mate, both small fortunes in their day. An experienced seaman on *Milton* received $769, a novice seaman, $571. Even the smallest pay was a respectable sum, much more than a farm hand could hope to earn in several years.

There seemed no limit to the booming industry. In 1846,

of the 966 whalers on the high seas, 736 of them were Yankee ships. The Yankee whaler was known in every major port of the world. San Francisco and Hawaii became whaling centers. At the peak, sixteen thousand were employed in an industry that grossed five million dollars a year, but by the middle of the century, the ships had to cruise longer and search farther. Some came home with empty barrels. The unleashed slaughter was slowly killing the industry.

Had it not been for the Civil War, American whaling might have died a lingering death. Instead, the end was sudden. The Confederate cruiser *Shenandoah* captured and burned twenty-five whalers soon after the war began. Eventually the Confederate toll reached fifty ships. Later in the war, Union forces purchased forty whalers, loaded them with rock, and sank them in shipping channels to block southern ports. When peace came, whaling did not revive, and soon petroleum pumped from the earth was providing fuel for lamps, a fuel both cheaper and cleaner than whale oil. New England ports and San Francisco still managed to send a few whalers to sea, but the ships had to range far north to find success.

Arctic ice caused severe losses. In 1871, thirty-three whalers were caught in the ice north of Alaska and abandoned by their crews. Five years later, ice destroyed twelve more whalers. In August of 1888, a gale north of Point Barrow destroyed five ships. In 1897, an unusually early freeze caught eight poorly provisioned whalers in the same area. It left 265 crewmen to face the Arctic winter. They were saved from starvation through a daring, overland rescue led by Lieutenant David H. Jarvis of the U.S. Revenue Cutter Service, forerunner of the Coast Guard.

Men continued to sail into the Arctic even in this century, but they found poor hunting. The last square-rigged vessel sailed from New England in 1920. Shore stations continued to process whales hauled in by steam catchers, but these operations also dwindled. In 1971 when the Department of Interior ordered an end to commercial whaling in the United States there was but one small San Francisco firm still in operation. A more significant part of the department's action was a ban on the import of whale products, particularly whale meat canned as pet food. This may discourage hunting by other nations of the world.

At its present pace, the hunt cannot continue long. In 1970 whale factory ships and shore stations processed a total of forty-two thousand whales, of which 84 percent were taken by Russian and Japanese ships. These countries process whale meat for human consumption. They say whaling is a vital source of protein for their people, but the whales taken are small by old standards, and the cost of the hunt increases yearly. Perhaps economic forces will end whale hunting before the hunters end the whale.

The native hunters, who took seals for centuries, made no drastic inroads in seal populations. Commercial hunters did. And while native hunters wasted little, the commercial hunters usually sought one thing, the skins. The native, hunting the seals through the ice, as described earlier, gave the seals a sporting chance. Commercial hunters had neither the patience nor the skill to stalk a seal on the ice or stand still as a stone above a breathing hole. The commercial sealers found the breeding grounds. There, with clubs or rifles, men would wreak wholesale slaughter. Skinners followed the attack, while flocks of gulls and other scavengers shrieked and wheeled overhead. In a few days of frantic work, a colony of seals could be wiped out.

Like whales, seals evolved from land animals. The bone structure of seal flippers shows that they once served as legs. On land, the seals continue to use their flippers for awkward walking. In the water, seals swim with marvelous speed and grace.

Some species can remain under water twenty, thirty, even forty minutes as they feed on fish, crabs, or other creatures. Some can reach depths of two thousand feet. Scientists have just begun to understand how seals manage these feats.

Seals have a large amount of blood, about one and a half times more in proportion to weight than most land mammals, which enables them to store a reserve supply of oxygen in their systems. In addition, seals reduce their heartbeats in a dive. On the surface, the heart beats 150 times per minute. In a dive, this drops to ten beats per minute, thus cutting blood circulation to a minimum and conserving oxygen. Seals also have a high tolerance for carbon dioxide. A man can hold his breath little more than two minutes before carbon dioxide in his system forces him involuntarily to breathe.

Seals also have remarkable protection against cold. The fur traps insulating air bubbles, and the blubber beneath the skin blankets in the body heat. To prevent loss of heat through the thin, often furless flippers, the seal can close off the blood vessels in these extremities.

Some seals can swim in short spurts up to eighteen miles an hour, a speed that is often vital in escaping sharks or killer whales. Seals can also communicate under water with

distinctive squeaks and grunts, and there is strong evidence
that seals use a sonar system, enabling them to find food and
navigate around obstructions in the depths by bouncing
echoes off their squeaks and grunts through the water. Some
scientists say such a system is the only possible explanation
for the seal's remarkable ability to locate the breathing holes
it maintains in the Arctic ice.

There are many breeds of seals, and all except harbor
seals, some sea lions, the monk seal, and the fresh water seal
of Lake Baikal spend at least part of the year in polar waters.
The small ringed seal, never exceeding 250 pounds, lives in
the far north all year. This made it a mainstay for native
hunters who could count on the ringed seal in any season.
The northern fur seal, on the other hand, migrates with the
season, returning from southern waters each summer to
Arctic islands to breed and bear pups. The fur seal colony
on the Pribilof Islands in the Bering Sea is by far the largest.

The story of the fur seal, while it has a happier ending than
many, typifies the history of commercial sealing. This seal
has a coat of two layers: an outer layer of coarse, long hairs
and an inner layer of fine, short hairs. Before curing, workers
scrape the skin, cutting free the roots of the longer hairs.
When these are removed, the highly prized pelt of fine hairs
remains.

Fur seal hunting began in 1786 when Russian explorer
Gerasim Pribilof discovered the colony. During the eighty
years that followed, when the Russian fur industry spread
across the northern Pacific, taking sea otters as well as many
varieties of seals, the fur seal suffered heavy losses. The
harvest, figured conservatively, reached two and a half million pelts. Twice during the Russian era, in 1806 and again

in 1834, hunting ceased, not because of government control but because there were too few seals. Each time, the seal population managed to recover sufficiently to encourage return of the hunters, but when the harvest began to decline a third time, Russian hunters agreed to take only bachelor bulls. Since the fur seal is polygamous, with a healthy bull having up to fifty cow seals in his harem, there are many non-breeding bulls. Taking these did not curtail reproduction.

In 1870, after the United States purchased Alaska, an annual quota of 100,000 fur seals was imposed. For a time, this seemed to be preserving the population, but a new development arose in 1879: Russian, Japanese, Canadian, and American hunters began taking the fur seal at sea, thus avoiding the Pribilof quota. This was extremely wasteful, since about half of the seals that were shot sank before they could be hauled aboard ship; furthermore, the sea hunters made no distinction between cows and bulls.

In 1883, just four years after the sea hunting began, the Pribilof Islands harvest fell below the 100,000 quota. Seven years later, the fur seal industry collapsed. Only then did the various nations involved consider additional controls. The loss of the industry was sorely felt. For the United States, the government royalties collected from fur sealing had nearly equaled the $7,200,000 purchase price of Alaska. No hunting treaty could be agreed to until 1911 when Japan, Russia, Canada, and the United States jointly banned their hunters from taking seals at sea and ruled that the kill must be limited to males. The agreement was almost too late.

The seals, reduced to a pitiful few, had other enemies than man. Sharks and killer whales preyed on them. But the seals slowly gained in number. In 1943, for the first time in fifty-four years, the harvest reached the old quota of 100,000 pelts.

The northern fur seal was thus saved from the fate of its southern cousin, the Guadalupe fur seal, which once numbered in the millions along the western shores of North and South America. In addition to pelts, the Guadalupe seal yielded excellent oil. Hunting reached its peak late in the last century when three million pelts were taken in a seven-year period. Today, the only known colony on an island off Baja California numbers less than five hundred.

Other species are almost as rare. Some students of the Arctic fear the walrus is now headed for extinction. Its range has certainly been reduced.

Ohthere's expedition to the White Sea late in the ninth century provides the first record of a walrus hunt. He and five men easily killed fifty-six animals in two days. These huge beasts, twelve feet long and weighing a ton, are extremely clumsy on land and are unable to escape a lance or club.

Walrus tusks provided fine ivory and the hide, cut in strips and braided, made strong rope. Commercial hunters had no difficulty selling their harvest. The slaughter began off Norway, the Kola Peninsula, and western Scandinavia.

During the thirteenth century, the Norse colonies on Greenland sent walrus ivory to Europe. Some of this ivory served as the Greenlander's tribute to support the Crusades. In the sixteenth century, skippers sailing under the flag of the Muscovy Company often took side excursions to hunt walrus, and late in the century, after Barents's final voyage, the hunt spread to Bear Island, the Svalbards, and Novaya Zemlya.

Late in the eighteenth century, after whalers had depleted

the herds in the region of the Svalbards, they turned to hunting walruses. One captain boasted of throwing up a pen around the beasts, holding them so his men could kill at their leisure. The walrus had no chance. The slaughter depleted the animals and finished the industry they supported. In 1860, a hunter returned from a Spitsbergen expedition to report in disgust that he had killed just one walrus. The hunt turned eastward beyond Novaya Zemlya into the Kara Sea. The walruses there held out remarkably well despite a harvest of a thousand or more animals a year. The hunters claimed the population was holding. This slaughter continued until 1930, when the herds suddenly diminished. In a decade, the number taken dropped to a pitiful twenty beasts a year. Today, in Arctic waters from Norway to Central Siberia, the walrus is rarely seen.

When the American colonies began, hunters found walrus herds in the Gulf of St. Lawrence and off the coast of Nova Scotia. Within a few years, the animals retreated into Davis Strait and Baffin Bay, and again, as the whale populations diminished, whalers turned to walruses.

Commercial hunting off Greenland and Baffin Island continued into this century. One trading company collected four thousand hides in a single year, but this does not fully represent the number killed, for many hunters shot the beasts at sea. No more than one-fourth could be recovered before they sank. In 1940, native Greenlanders who depended on the walrus for hides and blubber reported their catch had dropped by half. A closed season has since been imposed, limiting the hunt to four months each year. Under this control, the walruses of Greenland appear to be making a slow recovery.

On the other side of North America, walrus hunting in the Bering and Chukchi seas began with the Russian fur trade. From 1799 to 1857, Aleut and Eskimo hunters employed by Russians killed more than half a million walruses. During the peak harvest, hunters were disappointed if they took less than a hundred animals a day, but in 1883 a hunter taking eighteen in one day considered himself lucky. Early hunters on the Pribilof Islands reported walruses by the thousands. The last walrus was killed there in 1891. Today none are found south of Alaska's Nunivak Island. With depletion of the herds and with a drop in demand for ivory, survivors of the once great walrus populations may live on.

Man's interest in the unique creatures has begun to shift from exploitation to scientific study. Our knowledge has improved. At one time, men thought the tusks, some as long as two feet, served only to help the walrus pull itself onto the ice. In fact, the scientific name for the walrus, *Odobenus,* means one who walks with his teeth. We know now that the primary use of the tusks is to dig clams and other mollusks, the chief food of the walrus. The walrus uses his stiff whiskers as strainers to separate crushed shell from meat. The walrus pup grows quickly on its mother's rich milk, but the tusks, enabling the pup to feed for itself, develop so slowly that weaning is delayed until the walrus is two years old.

Walruses, when they haul out to rest or gather in breeding colonies, prefer ice to land. This preference may have been developed only during recent centuries to evade hunters. The ice, less accessible to man, is a safer haven for the walrus. However, the walrus cannot travel far on ice or land and must have open water if he is to feed. Pilots of U.S. Air Force planes patrolling the ice daily off northern Alaska have discovered that the walrus is an uncanny forecaster. If herds are spotted on the ice, it means a certain break-up of the pack can be expected within a few hours. For all his technology and refined instruments, man cannot yet predict ice changes nearly as well as the walrus.

While commercial walrus hunting has practically ceased, seal hunting continues. Currently, the harp seal is the most heavily hunted, and the hunt brings louder and louder public outcry each season.

The harp seal is one of the smallest seals. Adults, about six feet long, rarely weigh more than four hundred pounds. Adult pelts are light gray with a darker, harp-shaped saddle over the back. The pup's pelt is snow white, making it prized in fashion markets of the world.

The latest estimate puts the combined herds of the White Sea, the Greenland Sea, and the waters off Newfoundland at five million seals. Half a million, mostly pups, are killed annually. During the pupping season, beginning in February, hunters march out on the sea ice to club seals. A newborn pup weighs twenty-five pounds. It doubles its size in two weeks, but remains relatively helpless, particularly when its mother has left to dive for food. On the approach of a hunter, the pup will either make a pitiful attempt to crawl away or it will freeze in terror. The hunter can kill with little more effort than one swing of his club.

Harp seal hunting began two hundred years ago, and the number taken annually has increased. The population so far seems to be holding steady, but the public outcry is not so much against endangering the species as it is against the hunting method. Few people seeing a photo of a pup seal's innocent face can help being moved to compassion, and some argue that the clubbing is degrading to the spirit of the hunter. One hunter recently said, in defending his trade, that he at least made sure the pup was dead before he skinned it, suggesting that others are not so careful.

Sealing continues as a major industry for Newfoundland. In 1970 alone, 245,000 pelts were taken there with a total value of $1,750,000. The Canadian government has been reluctant to curtail such an industry, but in 1972 a one-year restriction was placed on hunting by ship and by plane in the Gulf of St. Lawrence. Since most hunting was done by a sealing fleet in this area, it was expected that limiting the kill to land-based hunters would lower the season's harvest substantially. The government, however, has not adopted any long-range policy that would limit hunting.

The polar bear, though not a marine mammal in the same sense as whales and seals, spends most of its life on or in the Arctic Ocean. It too has suffered from the onslaught of modern man. The ice king, symbolic of the far north, much prefers ice to land. Except for a she bear with cubs, polar bears are solitary nomads. Their only company is the Arctic fox which follows to feed on the bear's leavings.

Though they cannot dive as deep as a seal or stay under as long, bears are at home in the water. Scientists recorded one case in which a bear swam two hundred miles nonstop. On rare occasions, a polar bear will come ashore to eat berries, but their main diet consists of seals and fish.

Canadian, Russian, Danish, Norwegian, and United States zoologists working under an international program have been trapping, weighing, tagging, and releasing bears in the Arctic since 1965 to learn more of their range and habits.

Dr. Charles Jonkel of the Canadian Wildlife Service so far
holds honors for the biggest bear. He trapped a male weighing 1,450 pounds.

Though they do wander far, the bears are not circumpolar.
There are distinct stocks that limit themselves to specific
territory. Blood samples and skull measurements of Alaskan
bears differ from those of Svalbard. The best estimate by
scientists puts the total polar bear population at a little under
twenty thousand, with only about twenty-five hundred in
Alaska.[11] The numbers are declining. In the first four years
of the study program, hunters killed 103 tagged bears. Probably more were killed that were not reported. The hunters
of Alaska are now killing fewer bears, because they are be-
coming more and more difficult to find, mainly owing to the
increased accessibility of the Arctic. An executive on a long
weekend can fly from New York to Kotzebue, Alaska, hire a
plane and a guide, and be over the Arctic ice in a few hours.
Kotzebue citizens, who refer to their town as the Polar Bear
Capital of the World, get most of their income from white
hunters. There were thirty-two guiding teams, each with one
or more planes, working out of Kotzebue in 1970. Hunters
pay from $4,000 to $7,000 for a team on the average weekend.

The plane flies the hunter over the ice until tracks are seen.
It does not take long for the speeding plane to follow the
tracks to a bear. Though it is illegal, a second plane sometimes herds the bear to a convenient spot where the first
plane can land the hunter. The hunter spends only a few
minutes on the ice, just long enough to shoot the bear and
assist in loading it onto the plane. Back in his office next day,
the hunter can boast of the bear rug or trophy that will soon
decorate his den.

So far, efforts to halt this "sport" have not cleared the Alaskan legislature. Organizations, such as the Daniel Boone Club, which keep records of sportsmen's trophies, no longer list polar bears. The clubs have ruled the method an unfair contest. Meanwhile, the annual polar bear kill declines. White hunters took twenty-six in 1968 and twenty-two the next year.

Eskimos still look upon the polar bear as the most challenging quarry. A young native who kills his first bear has proven his manhood. Annual native kill, though hard to estimate, is probably about a hundred.

If the history of sea animals offers any lesson to man it is restraint, but man has failed again and again to learn the simple lesson. Despite man's foolishness, some hope remains. The mammals show remarkable recovery powers when protected. Sea otters, once thought extinct, have returned to coastal California and the Aleutians. An international treaty protects them. The grey whale, practically wiped out by 1930, has recovered and resumed its seasonal migration from the Bering Sea down the coast of North America to its winter breeding grounds in the Gulf of California. Population estimates of the greys range up to eighteen thousand. They remain protected by treaty.

In time, perhaps man's wisdom will improve. Populations of many depleted species might be restored, and the whaling and sealing industries, under sensible controls, might once again provide wealth to man and satisfy his unending quest for adventure.

7

Animals and Ice

WHILE THE ARCTIC Ocean can support polar bears and herds of whales and seals, the land areas of the Arctic provide home for an even greater variety of life.

Hares, lemmings, and foxes occupy the Arctic year-round, hibernating through the winter and emerging in astounding numbers with the return of the sun. While the caribou moves south to escape winter's worst storms, the musk ox, one of the world's strangest beasts, roams the northern reaches of the Arctic shores through all seasons. Huge flocks of migratory birds come to the Arctic each summer to rear their young, but there is one bird that remains all year long, the ptarmigan.

Many northern animals, including the Arctic fox, the Arctic hare, and the snowy owl, have white fur or plumage for camouflage, but the ptarmigan's protective coloration is by far the most specialized. In winter, the ptarmigan blends so perfectly with snow or ice that a man may nearly step on one unwittingly. The bird waits until the last safe instant before rising with an explosion of snow and whir of wings.

Through spring and summer as snow and ice melt, exposing the browns and grays of the earth, the ptarmigan molts and its plumage becomes blotched with browns and grays. The male is slower to shed its white coat, a delay that serves well for the decoy duty he must perform. His white feathers catch the eye of predators such as the skua gull and falcon. The male draws these egg robbers and chick killers away from the nesting hen. At the end of the dangerous season, the male ptarmigan molts and gains a plumage that blends with the summer terrain.

Ravens—the scavengers found on all continents of the world but Antarctica—stay almost as far north as the ptarmigans, but as carrion, plant seeds, and animal droppings grow scarce during the depth of winter, the ravens are forced south for food.

Among the migratory birds of the Arctic, the snow bunting is the first arrival. In early spring, long before the snow has melted, male buntings appear, selecting and defending nesting territory. The females arrive about two weeks after the males. Sea birds appear with the spring thaw. By June, swooping, raucous birds fill the sky. Ducks, geese, gulls, plovers, murres, and auks migrate thousands of miles each season, but the champion flier is the Arctic tern which spends the summer in the Arctic and then flies south eleven thousand miles to take advantage of another summer, that of the southern hemisphere, at the Antarctic. Ross's gull, on the other hand, seems to prefer the northern winter. When summer ends, the Ross's gull leaves its nesting ground on the Siberian coast, flies east to Alaska, and then turns north to spend the dark season over the polar icecap where it dives for fish in the rare leads of open water.

The ivory gull is another year-round Arctic sea bird. It is very rare. American ornithologist George Miksch Sutton, who joined a scientific expedition to Bathurst Island in the middle of the Arctic Archipelago in 1969, saw sanderlings, snowy owls, greater snow geese, king eider, oldsquaw, red-throated loon, brant, purple- and buff-breasted sandpipers, and red phalarope, but he failed to see an ivory gull. It was not until Sutton and his friends stopped at Cornwallis Island on their way home that anyone saw this rare bird. A flock was feeding on the garbage-strewn shore near an Eskimo village.

Even more rare is the Eskimo curlew. This curved-beaked bird, smallest of the curlews, once numbered in the millions, but its migration from the Arctic to South America took it through heavily populated regions of North America. Unfortunately for the Arctic curlew, it had little fear of man and its meat was delicious. Commercial hunters, armed with sticks, could march through a resting flock at night and kill birds by the wagonload. By 1890, the curlew was scarce. Fifty years later, it was thought extinct, but in 1963 a few individuals were sighted in Texas during spring migration. The species may yet survive.

The most important land animal in the Arctic balance of
nature is the lemming. After spending most of the year beneath the snow, these animals emerge for the few weeks of
summer to feed on tender willow shoots and grass. The
lemmings become so numerous in some seasons that it is
nearly impossible to avoid stepping on them, and natives
practically have to give up trying to drive sledge teams. Dog
teams are so distracted by fresh lemming trails that they
cannot be kept on course. In the following summer, not a
lemming can be found. The population in most regions peaks
in a four-year cycle. In lean lemming years, starvation
threatens falcons, ermines, snowy owls, and foxes. These
predators switch attention to the Arctic hare, but its numbers
soon decline. As food grows scarce, the snowy owl flies south,
sometimes as far as the northern border of the United States,
but the owl does not fare well in the lower latitudes, mainly
because its white plumage makes it too conspicuous. So the
owl population also decreases.

The Arctic fox, well attuned to the lemming cycle, might
raise as many as twelve kits in a good lemming year, but in
poor years the vixen kills her kits soon after they are born.
In poor lemming years, ermines simply do not breed. For
men who trap ermines, a poor lemming year means little
income.

What controls the spectacular rise and fall of lemming
populations? The lemmings themselves. After a summer of
high population, a self-destructive urge to migrate drives the
lemmings. In the middle of winter, they will rise from their
burrows and fan out across the ice by the thousands. If open
water crosses their path, the small rodents will plunge into
it and try to swim. All but a few die from drowning or

exposure. Scientists believe food shortage or perhaps crowding prompts the migrations, but there may be other factors involved that man has as yet failed to recognize.

Unlike the lemming, caribou and musk ox populations do not fluctuate. They simply decline, and since the introduction of the rifle, the decline has been drastic, particularly for the caribou. Herds of caribou in the North American Arctic once numbered in the millions. Today there are about two hundred thousand animals. These survivors continue to follow the old trails of migration, grazing on moss and lichens along the Arctic shore in summer and retreating more than a thousand miles to the tree line and below in winter.

Caribou are closely related to reindeer of the Old World. One important difference is that reindeer are far easier to domesticate. Man has made several attempts to transplant herds of reindeer to Alaska and Canada. So far, the attempts have been disappointing. In 1920, a herd of two hundred thousand in Alaska seemed to promise the start of the valuable meat industry, but beef and sheep farmers of the lower forty-eight states, fearing competition, forced through an embargo on reindeer meat. The herd was sold to Canadian herdsmen who drove the animals to the tundra of the Mackenzie River delta. There, despite many difficulties, the venture is showing some promise. Annual meat production from the Mackenzie herd is expected to reach a million pounds by 1976, but even this cannot nearly match the reindeer industry of Siberia. There, the Russians claim today an annual yield of eight million pounds of meat.

Herds of domestic musk oxen may soon be found grazing in the Arctic. The musk ox, classified by science between a steer and a sheep, grows two coats of hair. Long hairs of the outer coat come so close to the ground that it appears that the animal wears a flowing skirt. The fine hair of the inner coat is one of nature's best heat insulators. Herds of musk oxen have been seen grazing on windswept slopes in apparent comfort when the thermometer showed −50° F.

It is the inner hair, finer than cashmere, that has prompted interest in domesticating the musk ox. Today, experiments are underway in Vermont where breeders are seeking to develop docile, disease-resistant strains. Many major textile firms are watching the experiment closely.

Native hunters killed the musk ox for meat as well as for its warm pelt. The hollow horns, which curve down the side of the beast's head in the shape of a bonnet, were also valued by Eskimos. With just a little carving, a horn could be turned into a fine spoon. Even before introduction of the rifle to the north, native hunters had little difficulty taking the musk ox. Instead of running from its enemies, the beast stands in defiance. If in a herd, the animals will form a defensive ring, with the young and weak inside and the strong outside. While this might intimidate a wolf, it made an easy target for native spear hunters.

One of the few instances for which the native hunter is to blame is the decline of the musk ox. The animals were once circumpolar and their bones have been found as far south as Kentucky. Today, musk oxen are found only in the northern reaches of Greenland and the Arctic Archipelago. Here, under government protection, the survivors appear to be maintaining a stable population.

Other instances of animal depletion for which native hunting has been blamed are prehistoric, and the blame may not be justified. A breed of giant beaver, a giant moose, a camel, a big-horned bison, a horse, and a wooly mammoth have all left their bones in the Arctic. All are extinct today. No one is certain why.

The mammoth survived until well after the end of the last Ice Age. Cossack ivory hunters collected the tusks of some forty thousand of these beasts from mammoth graveyards all along the Siberian north. Forty mammoth carcasses have been found in various states of preservation, frozen in the tundra. The elephant of the north stood about nine feet high at the shoulders, had long skirts of coarse hair and large, curving tusks. In museum displays of Chinese art today, many of the intricate ivory carvings were made from mammoth tusks collected in Siberia by Cossack traders.

Most of the frozen animals discovered so far were evidently trapped in bogs or pinned under caving river banks. Bogs and cave-ins, however, could not alone cause extinction of a species. What did?

For many years, scientists believed the mammoths and other prehistoric mammals of the north died off because of some abrupt change in climate, but today this theory seems invalid. Examination of stomach contents among the frozen mammoths shows a diet of moss, lichens, and grass little different from tundra vegetation today. There has evidently been no abrupt change. There has certainly not been an era of hot weather. The frozen beasts would not have been preserved in that case. The big animals had no place to hide on the open tundra, and it would have been easy for bands of men to herd the mammoths into low, boggy ground for wholesale slaughter.

Does this explain what happened to the other vanished mammals of the north? The horse was certainly swifter, more elusive than the mammoth. The giant beaver was certainly more difficult to hunt. There is a mystery here that science has not begun to solve. Perhaps there was some abrupt change in Arctic conditions we do not yet suspect, a change connected somehow with the Ice Age itself. Our understanding of that great transformation is extremely limited.

In the past fifty years, man has learned much about the polar ice. Sea ice has been measured and its seasonal fluctuation has been charted. Glacial ice, including the great icecap of Greenland has been watched closely and much data has been gathered on rate of movement, melting, and thickness. Even permafrost, that mixture of ice, sand, and gravel hidden beneath the tundra, has begun to yield its secrets, but despite all the concentrated studies, man must have more information before he can determine the precise influence of polar ice on weather and climate, and the mystery of the Ice Age may never be solved.

The great sheets of ice that covered much of Europe, Asia, and North America began their retreat just twenty thousand years ago, hardly the blinking of an eye to geologists who trace the story of the earth through millions of years. What caused the massive advance of ice? Will it occur again? If so, when? Scientists can only guess at the answers. Some experts are not certain the Ice Age is over. It may be that we are enjoying today one of the temporary retreats that studies show occurred at least four times during the million years of the last Ice Age.

Actually, there have been many previous Ice Ages as scars in old rocks show. The recurring ice, according to one theory of science, prevented insects or reptiles from gaining lasting dominance on earth. As cold killed off or restricted development of these forms, mammals emerged. And it might be that the harsh environment of ice and cold forced evolution of that craftiest mammal of all—man.

For several years following *Fram's* historic voyage, polar scientists believed the northern ice was rapidly melting. Nansen and his men drilled a test hole near the ship and found the ice to be forty-three feet thick. No explorer since has found a floe thicker than twelve feet. Today, scientists are fairly sure that Nansen's measurement was taken through a pressure ridge. We now know that these ridges not only mound up on the surface of the ice where floes are forced together, but they also build down in great, submerged veins. Instead of a rapid melting, the polar ice appears to be relatively stable. There remains, however, much disagreement on trends.

For instance, Bernt Balchen, a polar flier and veteran ice student, predicted in 1968 that the polar icecap would be gone in from ten to twenty years. He based this on measurements taken by himself and others over several years, measurements which showed a rapid decline. Balchen's prediction has been loudly disputed by other scientists who claim the measurements failed to allow for normal, seasonal variations. Dr. Joseph O. Fletcher of the University of Washington has made studies which counter Balchen's findings. Fletcher points to history, claiming a retreat in ice from the ninth to the thirteenth centuries allowed Norse settlement of Iceland and Greenland, and that an advance in ice coincided with the disappearance of the Greenland colonies. There have been minor fluctuations since, but heavy icing which occurred around Iceland in 1970 suggests to Fletcher that the polar ice is once again on the increase.

Recently, great fears have been voiced, particularly among conservationists, that automobiles, jet aircraft, and factories are increasing the proportion of carbon dioxide in the atmosphere to such an extent that world climate will change drastically. Carbon dioxide lets solar radiation pass readily through the atmosphere, but it retards the loss of heat reflected from the earth's surface. It acts much like the glass roof of a greenhouse. Despite the industrialization of the past decades, it does not appear today that this greenhouse effect has changed, and if Fletcher's view is correct about increasing polar ice, it appears that other, stronger factors control world weather and climate. Man's ability to pollute the air, in fact, must take second place to nature's achievements.

In 1912, when the eruption of Katmai Volcano on the Alaskan Peninsula raised a globe-circling cloud of dust into the atmosphere, so much of the sun's heat was blocked from reaching the earth that glaciers of the Northern Hemisphere began to grow at an alarming rate. Fortunately, "the little ice age," as it was called, stopped as soon as skies cleared.

One theory has it that ice ages were caused by volcanic activity. While the earth was certainly more volcanically active than it is today, there is not enough correlation between periods of eruption and ice ages to give the theory much support. Another theory holds that the earth, in its regular migration through our galaxy, passes periodically through a cloud or clouds of cosmic dust. Because the dust filters the sun's rays, the earth cools and ice advances. The cosmic dust theory neatly explains the periodic return of the ice. The theory has many supporters.

There are several other Ice Age explanations, however, and one seems just as logical as the next. Take the Ewing-Donn theory: Maurice Ewing and William L. Donn, of Columbia University's Lamont Geological Laboratory, figure that fluctuating ocean levels are responsible for the advance and retreat of ice. They say that during an Ice Age great volumes of water are trapped on land in the form of ice. As this land ice increases, the level of the world's oceans falls. Because the Arctic Ocean has just a few openings to the warmer waters of the rest of the globe, a falling water level means that less and less warm water flows into the Arctic. The Arctic Ocean cools and eventually freezes over. When this happens, Ewing and Donn say, land ice begins to retreat. The reason is that the land ice is fed by storms born over an open ocean. An ice-covered ocean cannot yield enough moisture through evaporation to produce the necessary snowfall for a land-blanketing ice sheet. Of course, as the land ice melts, water levels gradually rise once more. As this trend continues, more and more warm water flows into the Arctic until the sea ice once again melts. Then the stage is set for the start of a new Ice Age.

Ewing and Donn are thus saying that a new Ice Age is inevitable, and that the Arctic today may be at a critical turning point. It is no surprise then that scientists want to learn all they can about polar ice.

Fletcher is currently organizing a massive study of the ice of the Arctic Ocean. The United States and Canada have already endorsed the project and will finance it. Before work begins in 1973, however, it is hoped that Japan and Russia will also support the work with funds and scientists. Called the Arctic Ice Joint Experiment, its main purpose will be to learn enough about current heat exchange, melting rates, wind and ocean currents, and evaporation to bring about a substantial improvement in weather forecasting. This knowledge alone, Fletcher declares, will pay for the three-year project many times over.[12]

Scientists of the joint experiment will depend heavily on the recently developed science of micrometeorology, and they will work largely from ice stations far out on the polar icecap. The micrometeorology method calls for readings within inches of the ice or water surfaces. These readings show what goes on in the critical areas where air, ice, and water meet and give a new insight into the imperfect science of weather forecasting.

Use of ice stations in polar exploration was pioneered by Storker Storkerson, a member of Vilhjalmur Stefansson's extended expedition in the Arctic. In 1918, Storkerson and his men camped on an ice floe for several days as it drifted across the ocean for some four hundred miles northwest of the Arctic Archipelago. Without the labor of travel, the men were free to take repeated soundings of the ocean floor and compile much more complete weather information than they had been able to gather when on the trail. The venture, however, was limited by shortage of supplies.

In 1926, Nansen proposed that the supply problem could be met by aircraft, but it was eleven years before his suggestion was put to test, and it was done by Russians rather than Norwegians. Four large ski planes landed at 89° 25' north latitude with cargoes of food, scientific instruments, fuel, tents, and camping gear. When the planes took off again, four men remained on the ice. The ice party, led by Ivan D. Papanin, spent nine months on a drifting floe, taking soundings, water samples, and weather data and collecting microscopic diatoms and small shrimp from the sea. The same current that had carried *Fram* out of the ice carried the Russians to the east coast of Greenland. There, as their floe began to break up, an icebreaker met them and took the men and their valuable collection of data home.

Russia has been in the ice-station business almost continually since that first venture. The biggest undertaking came in 1948 when two hundred temporary stations were established across the Arctic Ocean to map the ocean floor. The most spectacular discovery was the Lomonosov Ridge, a ten-thousand-foot-high submarine mountain range running from Ellesmere Island to the Novosibirskiye Islands. We now know that Lomonosov is the middle of three parallel ridges crossing the Arctic. Alpha Ridge to the west is a broken series of peaks and canyons while the Arctic Mid-Ocean Ridge to the east is actually a deep trench bounded on each side by jagged peaks. This is an extension of the formation that runs north and south through the Atlantic. Russian soundings showed depths of twelve thousand feet and more in the valleys between the Arctic ridges.

Through the years since Papanin and his men returned from the north, Russia has established a succession of seventeen long-range ice stations. Tents have been replaced by insulated, prefabricated houses, and nothing is spared in food and comfort for the station scientists.

While Russia has dominated in maintaining drift stations on floes, the United States has taken the lead in studies from ice islands. These huge masses of glacial ice broken from the ice shelf north of Ellesmere Island provide a far more permanent home than sea ice. United States Air Force fliers discovered ice islands soon after World War II. The first one seen was fifteen miles wide, eighteen miles long, and had banks rising twenty-five feet above the surrounding floes. Today, there are almost one hundred known ice islands in the Arctic. In 1952, the United States established a station on one of these islands one hundred miles from the North Pole. It was occupied continuously for nearly two years as it drifted south toward Ellesmere and then west to the Alaskan coast before turning north again.

Borings through the ice revealed fifty-two distinct layers of glacial silt. Some borings struck boulders. Others brought up dead plants. Scientists estimated the ice was two thousand years old. The United States has operated several other stations on both islands and floes since its first venture. Much has been learned about the formation of sea ice.

We know that the surface of the sea begins to freeze over when its temperature drops to 28° F. This is four degrees lower than the freezing point of fresh water. It is the salt that lowers the freezing point of the sea, and as the salt or salinity varies, the freezing point varies. Off the Siberian Coast, for instance, where huge rivers dump fresh water into the ocean, ice forms earlier in the winter than in other regions.

As ice thickens, salt crystals gradually leave it. Salt is heavier than ice, and by the time ice is a year old it can be melted to provide fresh water. All the salt crystals have gravitated out. When warmer weather returns to the Arctic, the fresh water produced by melting floes does not readily mix with the sea. If the weather is calm, a pool of fresh water collects beneath the floe. With a drop in temperature, this pool will freeze before the surrounding salt water. Floes thus have a tendency to rebuild from the bottom.

Working from ice floes, United States scientists have taken cores of the ocean floor. These show that an abrupt change took place in the Arctic from eighteen thousand to twenty-five thousand years ago, for the cores show two distinct layers. The top, recent layer is charged with the skeletal remains of foraminifera, a microscopic marine animal, while the bottom layer is composed of mud showing very little evidence of life.

United States scientists have also taken pictures of the ocean floor. These show a surprising amount of glacial debris scattered on the muddy surface, dumped there probably by ice islands. There is so much debris, however, that scientists are puzzled. There must have been many more ice islands than are known today.

Instead of leading to an explanation of the Ice Age, the core samples and the photographs so far have simply made the puzzle more complex. Much more study must be done to perfect our understanding of the Arctic and its history.

The Russians sometimes take an experimental view toward polar science, suggesting artificial ways to melt the icecap or alter currents. In light of our limited knowledge, the suggestions are often frightening. At one time, the Russians considered spreading coal dust on the ice to hasten heat absorption and bring on an early thaw. This might have benefited Russian shipping, but it also could have upset weather patterns in the Northern Hemisphere. Fortunately, the proposal has been abandoned. Other projects, however, are still being discussed. One would dam Bering Strait and pump warm Pacific water into the Arctic to encourage melting. Here again, the change could disastrously alter weather and climate. The Russians have long considered a dam on the Ob River to divert it to water-needy regions to the south. The reduction of fresh water flowing into the Arctic would change ice conditions and weather patterns.

The Russian projects may never come to pass, but scientists place the threat of such undertakings almost on a par with the threat of war. Flood and crop damage could reach billions. Population centers far down in the lower latitudes might have to be relocated.

Sea ice is but one concern of the experts. Arctic permafrost lies beneath vast stretches of tundra equal in area to the lower forty-eight states of America. At Point Barrow, the permafrost is one thousand feet thick. On Siberia's Taimyr Peninsula it is two thousand feet thick. The tundra, composed of matted plants, both living and dead, serves as an insulating blanket over the permafrost. In summer, the tundra thaws to a depth of little more than two feet. In winter, even this thin surface layer freezes. The seasonal thaw and freeze produce some of the Arctic's strangest features.

Summer melt water that fills deep cracks must expand when it refreezes. The only direction to expand is up. Mounds called pingos result. Some pingos rise hundreds of feet above the surrounding tundra and remain as permanent features for years. A similar process on a smaller scale patterns much of the tundra surface into polygon-shaped dykes. In some regions these polygons extend as far as the eye can see, a giant quilt across the surface of the land.

One might think that ground, frozen and snow-covered

eight months of the year, and lying on a foundation of permafrost, would be sterile. This is not the case. In summer, the tundra blooms with life. Botanists have identified four hundred species of lichens and seventy-five species of mosses above the Arctic Circle. There are two flowering plants related to the grasses and one related to the carnation. In slightly warmer, sub-Arctic zones, there are two thousand species of lichens, five hundred of mosses, and about nine hundred flowering plants. The scrubby Arctic willow, which reaches a height of six inches in one hundred years of growth, is the only tree of the far north.

Glacial ice of the Arctic is looked upon as the last of the Ice Age's great ice sheet. There are large glaciers in Alaska and several on the islands of the Arctic, but the biggest concentration of land ice is in the Greenland icecap. It is 600 miles wide, 1,600 miles long, and up to 2 miles thick. If this mass of ice should melt, the oceans of the world would rise 20 feet. The weight of the icecap has depressed the rock foundation so much that much of Greenland's interior is below sea level.

The monotonous plain of Greenland ice is broken only by nunataks—jagged peaks that rise mostly near the Greenland coast. Outflow glaciers ooze between these peaks to dump bergs into the sea. From 10,000 to 50,000 icebergs, equal in mass to 125 cubic miles, are produced by Greenland glaciers annually. Some of these bergs are a mile long and rise 300 feet above the water. Currents carry them south into the Atlantic shipping lanes. Some bergs have reached Bermuda and the Azores, but most melt before drifting so far south. The bergs remain a serious hazard. In 1912, after the *Titanic* struck a berg and sank with the loss of 1,500 lives, the International Ice Patrol was created. It is run by the United States Coast Guard and financed by 14 maritime nations. It is an efficient operation, using radar, air patrols, and regular radio alerts, but even so, disasters continue. In 1959, the Danish passenger ship *Hans Hedtoft,* returning from her maiden voyage to Greenland, struck a berg and sank before any rescue vessel could reach her. None of her 95 passengers and crewmen could be saved.

Near the top of Greenland's icecap, which rises to 10,827 feet, the United States Army has built Camp Century. It is an underground city of chambers and tunnels carved out of the ice. Here, scientists can live in relative comfort some 800 miles from the North Pole, and they are as close to their work as a man can be. Borings into the ice have brought up samples 3,000 years old. The age can be found by isotope dating. Heavy oxygen, an isotope, increases in the atmosphere during the summer. The snow that falls during summer thus has more heavy oxygen than winter snow and the ice formed from the packed snow has seasonal layers. These layers show up clearly when the ice is examined under a spectroscope.

There is work for biologists as well as ice experts at Camp Century. Colonies of primitive life have been discovered in the ice. These appear as cylindrical holes ranging from an inch to three feet in diameter. At the bottom of these holes, sometimes two feet deep, the ice is stained with a mixture of dust, microscopic plants, and a multicelled animal called *rotifer,* distant relative of the earthworm. The colonies, dormant most of the year, grow under the summer sun, and the heat produced by their growth melts the holes in the ice.

These colonies can be transplanted. A handful placed on bare ice melted a hole one foot deep in ten days. Scientists have also found a wingless flea and another variety of worm living on the Greenland icecap. The flea lives on pollen blown from distant plants. The worm lays eggs which hatch in the middle of the Arctic winter. These primitive life forms of the ice may be living samples of the beginnings of life on earth. They demonstrate an adaptability that convinces some scientists that life on other planets of the universe is almost certain.

8

Scientists Cooperate

EXPERTS OF MANY nations have just recently come together to study such things as polar bears and polar ice, but an international effort to solve the mystery of the Aurora Borealis of the north and the Aurora Australis of the south began in the last century.

The effort finally brought results. Today we know the cause of the brilliant lights that flash in polar skies and, as is typical of scientific inquiry, the explanation raises many new questions. Our understanding of aurora has broadened our curiosity about magnetism, cosmic radiation, and evolution of life. As with aurora studies, the new questions can best be approached through cooperation of all specialists and pooling of all knowledge. The aurora studies set the pattern for such cooperation.

Written record of aurora appeared in Roman times. In those days men said the gods were angry or the sky was on fire. There was no other explanation. The first step in solving the mystery did not come until the sixteenth century when English physician William Gilbert found that the lines of force around a magnet and the lines of force around the earth took the same essential shape. This magnetic field arched wide at the equator and pinched in at the poles. A century later, English astronomer Edmund Halley found through study of compass variation that the magnetic poles were actually located several hundred miles from the geographic poles. Neither Gilbert nor Halley, however, saw any connection between magnetism and aurora.

The link was not discovered until 1741, a year after Halley's death. Two Swedish scientists, Anders Celsius and Olav Peter Horter, observing aurora one March evening, were startled to discover that the needle of their compass swung several degrees each time the skies flashed. The discovery caused much discussion and prompted collection of more detailed data on magnetism. There were abrupt fluctuations in the earth's magnetic field. Sometimes these magnetic storms were so violent that ships' compasses became useless. What caused these disturbances, no one could say.

In 1859, English astronomer Richard C. Carrington recorded man's first observation of a solar flare. It was followed within hours by a violent magnetic storm. For several years, scientists failed to consider the two phenomena as connected, but then in 1874 the scholarly Hermann Fritz of Switzerland's Polytechnic Institute published a revealing report. Through much correspondence and exhaustive search of old records, Fritz collected every report of aurora for the past 174 years. The tables he compiled showed that Aurora Borealis and Aurora Australis occurred simultaneously, and moreover that they were most frequent during periods of sun-spot activity, when the sun sent up its awesome flares. If aurora were linked with sun-spot activity, and aurora were linked with magnetic storms, then logic said sun spots and magnetic storms were somehow connected.

Further light did not come to the mystery until the science of electronics dawned.

Meanwhile, Karl Weyprecht, one of the leaders of an Australian expedition that discovered Franz Josef Land, told the German Scientific Medical Association in 1875 that charting a new cape or bay might be significant, but it was not nearly as important as increasing man's knowledge of weather, magnetism, and the aurora. Such information, said Weyprecht, could best be collected by an international effort. Thus was born the First Polar Year.

Set for 1882, with eleven nations participating, the program called for most of the forty observation stations to be established above the Arctic Circle. The United States established a station at Point Barrow and another on Ellesmere Island. The latter, under command of Army Lieutenant Adolphus W. Greely, met disaster when ice blocked return of a supply ship. It took three years for the party to be rescued, and then only six of the original twenty-five men had escaped starvation.

The First Polar Year gathered additional data on aurora,

but it brought man no closer to a solution. In 1890, however, Norway's Kristian Birkeland, a pioneer in electronics, charged a sphere of metal with a magnetic field similar in shape to that of earth's. When the sphere was placed inside a vacuum tube and bombarded with electrons, a pale glow of light flickered at the top and bottom of the sphere. Carl Störmer, one of Birkeland's colleagues, carried the tests further and found that charged atomic fragments such as electrons spun in a circle upon striking a magnetic field at right angles. Since the earth's magnetic field is curved, fragments reaching it from the sun's radiation would rarely strike at right angles. They would enter the field obliquely and go spiraling off toward the poles. The electrons would be trapped by the earth's magnetic field with the greatest concentrations above the poles.

Störmer had come very close to solving the mystery of the aurora, but his studies at the time attracted little attention. Scientists had begun to plan a Second Polar Year. It took place in 1932 with forty-four nations participating. For the first time simultaneous photographs from various locations were taken of aurora. Also for the first time, scientists coordinated observation of radio transmission. They discovered that radio waves did unpredictable things during periods of magnetic storm. Did radio, too, have some link with aurora?

Unfortunately, many records collected during the Second Polar Year were lost or left unsorted because of World War II, but very soon after the war ended, talk about a third international effort began. Then, in 1950, came a new aurora discovery.

Alan B. Meinel, an astronomer at Yerkes Observatory in Wisconsin, had long been trying to match aurora light with the light of an element on the spectrum. Each element gives off its own distinctive light, but the light of the aurora matched none of them. Aurora light seemed to be produced by elements unknown to man. Meinel solved this enigma. Much of the light, he found, was produced by fragments of the hydrogen atom and atoms of other gases. These fragments were speeding toward earth so fast that the wave length of light they produced was compressed. It was much like the sound-wave distortion from the whistle of a speeding train. The whistle sounds high as the train approaches the listener, but the pitch drops abruptly as the train speeds away. Meinel calculated that the hydrogen nuclei, one of the particles involved in producing aurora light, had to be traveling 2,100 miles per second.

While Meinel was doing his work, another scientist was trying to find out what it was that caused fragments of the earth's atmospheric gases to speed so fast. At the time James A. Van Allen, on the staff of Johns Hopkins University, was a rocket researcher. He thought if enough rockets could be sent aloft with the proper testing equipment the answer to the speeding fragments might be found. Van Allen generally gets credit for proposing a third polar year, a program that eventually grew into the 1957–58 International Geophysical Year. Fittingly, one of the most significant discoveries of the IGY bears his name today—the Van Allen Radiation Belts.

Rockets fired above the stratosphere by the United States and other nations during IGY revealed "hot" bands of radiation. Early in the program, the geiger counters on some of Van Allen's rockets jammed because the radiation was so high. It was 1,000 times greater than expected, equal to

160,000 charged particles striking each second a surface the size of a standard postage stamp. These bands or belts of radiation were far above the earth's atmosphere at the equator, but the earth's magnetic field brought them down at the poles so that the fast moving particles collided with gases. The collisions sent atomic fragments of these gases speeding across the sky, causing various colored lights. Just as the gas in a neon tube glows when charged with electricity, so do the gases of the sky glow when struck by charged particles of the Van Allen Belts. Solar flares greatly multiply the number of charged particles in the belts and thus multiply the number of collisions in polar skies. Increase in radiation from solar flares increases the thickness of the Van Allen Belts. This change plays havoc with radio communication and magnetism. Radio beams bounce off the under layer of the belts. As the thickness of the belts changes, their elevations change, and the reflective pattern of the radio beams becomes confused. Understanding of the relationship between Van Allen Belts and magnetism is not so clear.

The traditional theory on magnetism holds that it is caused by the molten iron surging within the hot core of the earth. The so-called dynamo theory does not make clear why the earth's magnetic field has reversed direction, even lapsed several times in the geological past. Scientists are wondering today if the Van Allen Belts might have a governing influence on magnetism. The belts are believed to shield the earth from much harmful radiation, particularly X-rays from the sun. Since the belts are formed by the magnetic field, they would be expected to vanish when magnetism lapses. Marine biologists have found that the extinction of certain microscopic animals coincided with lapses in magnetism.

Was this due to radiation, or did the magnetic lapse some-how change the climate so much the animals could not sur-vive? Scientists cannot say.

Some students of evolution suggest today that an increase in radiation resulting from magnetic collapse may have been vital in the development of higher life. Radiation causes mutations, and mutations bring on new life forms.

Of course, discovery of the Van Allen Belts and the con-sequent solution of the aurora mystery was but one achieve-ment during the great cooperative undertaking of science. During IGY, Russia and the United States both launched artificial satellites, heralding the age of space exploration. In the Antarctic, as we shall see, scientists from many fields and many nations greatly expanded man's knowledge of the world's most remote continent. Other scientists did extensive work in the Arctic and explored above, across, and even under the polar ice. Outside of space travel, the journey under the ice ranks among the most remarkable of the modern age.

9

World in Balance

JUST BEFORE THE ship reached the North Pole, someone in the crew's mess turned off the juke box. Every one of the 117 officers and men knew from the arresting hush that the big moment was near. The only sound came from the steadily pinging sonar that automatically recorded the depth of the ocean below and the height of the ice roof above.

Then the captain, Commander William R. Anderson, spoke abruptly over the intercom: "Mark!" he said. The U.S. submarine *Nautilus* had reached the pole. It was 11:15 P.M. (Eastern Standard Time), August 5, 1958. A victory for the United States and its navy, yes, but most of all this was a victory for technology. Man had conceived, engineered, built, and sailed a ship that made him master of nature, a ship with awesome potential for both peace and war.

Nautilus was powered by an atomic reactor which allowed her to cruise 115,000 miles without refueling. The unique system was the brainchild of Admiral Hyman G. Rickover, chief of the Naval Reactors Branch of the Atomic Energy Commission. The power system, combined with an artificial atmosphere produced by bottled oxygen and carbon dioxide filters, made it possible for her to stay submerged for days on end. Her inertial guidance navigation, using the dead reckoning method refined by computer, made the ship independent of sun or star sights.

Moreover, *Nautilus* allowed men to be comfortable at the North Pole. Air conditioners kept the temperature at a constant 72° F and the humidity at 50 percent—shirt-sleeve weather. Most of the space in a conventional submarine is occupied by batteries to run the electric motors for submerged cruising, but the atomic submarine needed no batteries and her compartments were spacious. Fifty men could watch a movie in the messroom of the *Nautilus*.

The ship's historic voyage took her 1,830 miles under the ice from Point Barrow to the North Pole and on to the Greenland Sea in ninety-five hours. Her only real trouble came at the beginning when shallow water and deep-reaching walls of pressure ice blocked her first attempt in the Chukchi Sea. It was June, too early in the season. *Nautilus* retreated to Pearl Harbor. Anderson sent his navigation officer to Alaska to fly with survey planes and locate a break in the ice. He did not return to the ship until the summer thaw had opened most of the Arctic gateway. Then once more, the ship sped north.

Her sonar gear, designed for under-ice cruising by Dr. Waldo K. Lyon of San Diego's Naval Electronic Laboratory, again found the way barred. Anderson changed course to the southwest until he came to a submarine canyon off Point Barrow. There he pointed the ship north and ordered her down.

News of the *Nautilus's* success surprised the world. Secrecy had cloaked all preparations. Even the crew and most officers knew nothing of the mission until after the ship sailed.

One reason for secrecy was the Eisenhower Administration's fear that the American public could not stand the disappointment if the attempt, after advance publicity, should fail. Russia's success with Sputnik, man's first artificial satellite, had already shocked and humiliated the United States. A second reason was the Cold War. Tension between East and West was high. *Nautilus* might have to cruise close to the Siberian shore. There could be trouble. And though the *Nautilus* would contribute data for the International Geophysical Year, its prime mission was military.

During World War II, German U-boat skippers had learned to use the edge of the polar icecap as a haven from searching allied planes and ships. Even though these submarines had to surface periodically to charge their batteries, they could stay far enough under the ice to escape detection for hours. Atomic submarines, as the *Nautilus* demonstrated, turned the entire polar icecap into a potential battleground. With Polaris missiles, such subs could surface from icy ambush and launch atomic warheads at enemy targets seconds after hostilities began. The U.S. Defense Department believed this capability to be the greatest deterrent to a new world war since the development of nuclear bombs.

The department sent other submarines cruising in the wake of the *Nautilus.* In 1959, *Skate* broke through the ice and became the first ship to float on the surface of the Arctic Ocean at the North Pole. *Sargo,* in 1960, cruised beneath the polar icecap for thirty-one days and four hours on a course that led through Bering Strait, around the pole, and back to the Pacific. In the same year, *Seadragon* made a submerged west to east transit of the Northwest Passage in six days by way of McClure Strait and Lancaster Sound.

The voyages of the atomic submarines typified the prime interest of the United States in the Arctic. Our government has long looked upon the far north as the first front in a global war. So far, the armed forces of America have hired the most men and women, put up the largest payrolls, and undertaken the biggest construction projects in the North American Arctic. Our military concern goes back to World War II.

When the Japanese attacked Pearl Harbor late in 1941, Alaska was woefully unprepared for war. The few bases we had there depended on irregular shipping for supply. Military flying had hardly emerged from the pioneering stage. On June 3, 1942, with arming of Alaska barely begun, the Japanese bombed the United States Navy base at Dutch Harbor on Unalaska Island at the east end of the Aleutian chain. Within two weeks, enemy landing forces had occupied Attu and Kiska islands farther west in the chain. Radio communications and radio beacons were inadequate. Dutch Harbor's calls for help to a nearby fighter base went unheard throughout the attack. The Dutch Harbor transmitter was not strong enough to carry across an intervening ridge.

Fortunately, the Japanese did not know how weak we were. They failed to follow their advantage, and before long, in one of the most challenging struggles of the war, the Alaskan Peninsula and the Aleutian chain became an American stronghold. By 1943 there were fourteen thousand troops in Alaska.

Engineers had to learn to build bases on thick sand or gravel foundation to keep both air strip and buildings from sinking into the tundra. Ground crews had to devise quick methods for heating oil before flights and for draining it after flights. If left in the engines, oil would freeze. Pilots had to learn to fly in blinding fogs and blizzards with winds that sometimes peaked at one hundred miles an hour. As air and sea supply improved, work began on the 1,523-mile Alcan Highway from Seattle to Alaska. Army Engineers completed the project in an incredible eight months.

Meanwhile new bases were established and eventually bombing missions against enemy islands were flown from Adak, Amchitka, Shemya, Umnak, and Atka. Then, in bitter ground fighting (bitter both in climate and enemy defense), the United States Army drove the Japanese from Attu. A similar struggle was expected on Kiska, but when ground troops landed there they discovered that the enemy had evacuated under the cover of fog. The fighting was over, but Alaska has remained a military stronghold ever since.

Early in the 1950s, with tensions of the Cold War continuing to mount, the United States, in cooperation with Denmark and Canada, built a chain of radar stations 3,600 miles along the Arctic Circle from Alaska to Greenland.

The expensive project was designed to give enough advance warning so that planes could intercept an enemy air attack before it reached population centers in the lower forty-eight states.

This network, called the Distant Early Warning or DEW Line, became inadequate soon after completion. The threat of rockets required earlier alert. Huge radar towers, high as a thirty-story building, were constructed at Clear, Alaska, and at Thule, Greenland, to form the Ballistic Missile Early Warning System or BMEWS. Such construction projects challenged engineering ingenuity. The tundra would not support the weight of such towers. The answer was steam pointing. Stout, steel rods were driven deep into the permafrost behind a jet of steam. When the ground cooled, it froze solidly around the rods, providing a solid anchorage for the towers.

As the warning lines were being built, new bases for jet interceptors and anti-ballistic missile rockets went up across the Arctic. The northernmost base at Thule, Greenland, 950 miles from the North Pole today has a 14,000-foot runway and housing for 6,000 men. The United States Air Force keeps the jet interceptors there and at other Arctic bases in a constant state of preparedness. They can be aloft within seconds of an alert. Our Defense Department counts the radar systems, the air bases, and the rocket posts as further deterrents to global war.

The Arctic recently became the location for yet another military project which some described as a deterrent to war and others called a threat to peace.

On November 6, 1971, at a cost of 118 million dollars, the United States set off a five-megaton nuclear bomb a mile beneath the surface of Amchitka in the Aleutian Islands. The bomb, 250 times more powerful than the one dropped on Hiroshima, Japan, to hasten the end of World War II, was the 335th tested by the Atomic Energy Commission since the start of underground testing in 1957. Most nuclear bombs have been tested under the Nevada Desert, but the commission used its Amchitka site because this was the biggest bomb yet set off by the United States, and no one could say for sure how much damage it might do. The purpose was to test the warhead for the Spartan anti-ballistic missile. The Defense Department said the test was vital for national security. However, for several months before the test, protests raged both in the United States and abroad. Environmentalists feared earthquake and tidal wave damage, leakage of radiation, and loss of sea life from falling rocks and submarine concussion. Canada and Japan urged that the test be canceled. Eight conservation groups brought suit to stop the test, and the case went to the United States Supreme Court. Just a few hours before deadline, the court voted four-to-three to allow the government to go ahead. The popular protest was overruled.

As it turned out, the Amchitka bomb caused little evident damage, but the debate over the test focused new concern over the delicate balance of life in northern waters. Scientists consider the Arctic Ocean a sensitive ecosystem. A man-caused disaster such as a radiation leak or an oil spill could snuff out life. Even a slight change could destroy the microscopic plants beneath the ice. This would kill the shrimp and other small animals, and fish, seals, and whales would starve. The water would become sterile. The Arctic, smallest of the world's oceans, is almost land-locked. Pollution there can be expected to remain concentrated much longer than in the larger oceans with mighty, unobstructed currents.

During the Amchitka controversy, former Secretary of the Interior Walter J. Hickel declared that the real debate should center on testing itself. When will it all end? he asked.

We know the Russians have been conducting many tests, including several on Novaya Zemlya. One underground blast set off by the Russians in 1970 may have been a six-megaton bomb, bigger than the one tested at Amchitka.

Both Russia and the United States are reluctant to give up underground testing. It allows experimentation with new weapons, adjustment of bomb stockpiling, and development of totally different weapon concepts. But nothing the major powers can say in favor of testing bombs makes the activity anything besides a preparation for global war. Bomb tests then, while often an Arctic worry, are above all a world-wide concern.

Russia has many other military activities along its Arctic shore. Full details are not known in the West, but we do know Russia has built a radar detection system little different from our own BMEWS line. The Russians also maintain rocket sites and air fields across Siberia, and Russia undoubtedly has a fleet of atomic-powered submarines just as capable of destruction as our own.

But Russia's military activity in Siberia today is outstripped by peaceful industrialization and development of natural resources. It began soon after World War II. It continues to grow, a Siberian boom in wealth and activity that seems to have no end. Development of Spitsbergen's coal mines began late in the nineteenth century, and steel produced from the iron ore mined at Kiruna, Sweden, has long led in quality, but the Soviet production of coal, steel, oil, diamonds, gold, and other minerals has already many times exceeded these long-established Arctic industries. And Russia is far ahead of the United States and Canada in recognizing the potential of its Arctic resources.

Russia now relies on Siberia as the major source of lumber, natural gas, manganese, lead, nickel, cobalt, tungsten, molybdenum, bauxite, antimony, sulphur, and asbestos as well as the already mentioned coal, oil, gold, and diamonds. A program to harness the hydro-electric potential of Siberian rivers is well under way. One of the dams already completed is bigger than our Grand Coulee.

Russia does not readily give out figures on production and reserves to the rest of the world. Even so, information that is published usually becomes out-dated within days by increased production and new discoveries. Currently, a force of geologists is roaming Siberia searching for additional natural wealth. Their survey work, Soviet officials said in 1969, was barely a fourth completed.

The discoveries that have occurred are phenomenal. In 1960, geologists found that the swampy plains of the Ob River just east of the Ural Mountains, a forbidding territory in any season, hid a wealth in oil and natural gas. Despite the difficulties of drilling in a land of seasonal frost and swamp, the Russians hastened to tap the gas. The deposit, thought at first to contain 2.5 trillion cubic meters of natural gas, is bigger than anyone dreamed. By 1970 4 trillion cubic meters had been taken from the field, with no hint that the source might give out. Today a 2,600-mile pipeline, the world's longest for natural gas, carries the wealth of the Ob Valley discovery to Leningrad. The wells are shallow along the Ob, making operation cheap, and the petroleum pumped from the ground is of such high quality that it can be burned in Diesel engines without being processed in a refinery.

Since the Ob River discovery, thirty-five natural gas fields and at least twenty-eight oil fields, stretching from the Ural Mountains to the Sea of Okhotsk, have been discovered. In 1967, the total production of Siberian oil reached six million tons. This is evidently just the beginning. Russian economists say oil will be the foundation for the entire Siberian economy. Wealth from oil will be used to develop the many other resources.

There are many others. Gold began coming out of Siberian mines late in the seventeenth century. In 1745, an important new discovery was made in the Ural Mountains. Those mines continue in production today. Prior to the Russian Revolution, Siberian gold mines produced from two hundred to two hundred fifty tons a year. Since the revolution new deposits have been found on the Alden River, the Kolyma River, and up and down the Kamchatka Peninsula. While the United States gold reserves diminish annually, Russia's reserves continue to grow. The town of Magadan on the Sea of Okhotsk gives a good idea of the growth. In 1930, when gold was discovered on the nearby Kolyma, Magadan did not exist. Today it is a city of ninety thousand. In the beginning convict labor worked the gold mines, and the many banished to the mines linked Siberia with suffering, sorrow, and death. Siberia continued into this century as a land for both political and war prisoners, but today the attitude toward Siberia has changed. For the youth of Russia, Siberia holds the future. Geologists who have discovered rich deposits are among the recent heroes.

In 1955, diamonds were found just south of the Arctic Circle in the Yakut region. Today the deposits appear to be second only to those of South Africa. The first engineers and miners who arrived lived in miserable shacks where one man had to stay awake each night feeding a wood stove. Soon, however, barracks and houses rose. Today, the diamond town of Mirny has a population of forty thousand.

Norlisk, at 69° north latitude near the Yenisei River, gives yet another example of Siberia's rapid growth. Thirty years ago, it had fourteen thousand people. Today there are one hundred fifty thousand and the Norlisk production figures for copper, gold, cobalt, nickel, and coal continue to climb. Ore from some of the mines travels to smelters on conveyors through tunnels carved in the permafrost. From the smelters the metals go by rail to the port of Dudinka on the mouth of the Yenisei to await the summer shipping season. Norlisk, the most northern industrial city in the world, has fifty plants producing metals and chemicals. During the polar night, residents do not see the sun for six weeks, and blizzards sometimes rage for days on end. But the population of Norlisk is young. Most of her people are still in their twenties. The birth rate is high and children born there are said to be healthier than those born in milder climes.

Siberia's largest Arctic city is Murmansk on the Kola Peninsula where 226,000 live. The city grew to a major port in World War II when allied convoys carried vital supplies to Russia. Nazi planes and submarines sometimes sank more than half the ships before the convoy reached port. Murmansk remains an important shipping center as well as base for a large fishing fleet.

The natural resources found so far in the North American

Arctic are nearly as impressive as those of Siberia, but discoveries have lagged behind the Siberian finds and development has followed a different pattern. The vast oil reserve of
Alaska's North Slope, not discovered until 1968, may mark a
turning point in the western attitude toward resources in the
Arctic. All too often, our Arctic industries have been ex-
ploited rather than developed.

The gold rush of the last century is typical. Men went
north by the thousands. hoping to get rich fast and get out
fast in the fields along Alaska's Klondike River or in the
Yukon. Nome on the Seward Peninsula, capital for Klondike
prospectors, once had a population of twenty thousand.
Today there are twenty-seven hundred, mostly Eskimos,
living there, and the massive gold dredges brought north at
great expense stand as rusting hulks across the tundra, testament to the philosophy of boom or bust.

The Yukon strike of 1869 eventually brought eighty
thousand prospectors from fifty different nations to the far
north. The town of Dawson once had twenty-five thousand
residents and sixty-five stern-wheel steamers supplied the
territory during the peak days of commerce. By the beginning of this century, however, the dream of wealth began to
pass. Small mining companies merged or folded. Claims fell
into the hands of a few big investors. Independent prospectors had no place to go but home. Limited gold dredging
continued on the Yukon until 1966. By then, a quarter billion
dollars had been taken from the gravels. Very little of this
wealth stayed in the Arctic. The Yukon today, sapped of its
resources, is an impoverished district and the 846 residents of
Dawson have scant means of livelihood.

Rather than encourage permanent populations in the

north, the Canadians appear to continue a policy of limitation. The concentrated lead-zinc ores of Pine Point on Great Slave Lake, which were first mined in 1966, travel 437 miles by rail to smelters in British Columbia. Ore production is expected to reach 215,000 tons annually. If the smelting were done at the mines, however, shipping costs would be lowered and jobs would boost the economy of the dying region. Nearby Yellowknife, once another booming gold town, closed its last mine the same year the Pine Point mines opened. Today, all too many Yellowknife residents depend on welfare.

A few hundred miles to the north, at Great Bear Lake, uranium mines brought another economic boom. The bust came when the post-war market for uranium dropped. Again, those remaining at the mines need government help.

The mountain range forming the spine of Newfoundland, Baffin, and Ellesmere Islands is rich in iron ore. Geologists recently found deposits of high grade ore near Mary River in the north of Baffin Island, which they claim are the richest in the world. However, the short shipping season from Milne Bay, forty miles to the north, has delayed development. Mining of another rich iron ore deposit has begun at Schefferville at the border of Newfoundland and Quebec. Zinc, lead, and silver ores have been found near the coast of Ungava Bay on Hudson Strait where there is talk of harnessing the sixty-four-foot tides with hydroelectric plants. The power could be used to run smelters near the mines, a move that would reverse past policies.

There are many other resources known but not yet developed in the Canadian north. A reef of lead, zinc, and silver ore runs north in tidal water from Cornwallis Island.

Natural gas has been tapped by test wells on many other islands of the Arctic Archipelago and geologists believe future test holes will bring up oil. Canada's oil resources, so far, however, have been largely neglected.

Canada's first oil strike was on the Mackenzie River west of Great Bear Lake in 1920. The town of Norman Wells became the center for drilling activity and with World War II and rocketing demand for oil, the town boomed. Construction of the Canol pipeline began during the war, but the line was not completed until hostilities ended. Before the line was put in order, across the mountains to the Alcan Highway at Whitehorse, the Canadians decided to tear it up and sell the pipe for scrap. Today, most of the wells at Norman Wells are capped and the petroleum that is produced supplies only the needs of the small communities along the Mackenzie. Geologists, however, are convinced that a vast underground pool of oil, some 250 miles wide, extends from Norman Wells north to the Arctic Coast. The entire Canadian Arctic may have a reserve of 100 billion barrels. The decision to scrap the Canol pipeline must stand as a classic case of short-sightedness.

Development of the petroleum industry in Alaska, even though it started later, is today well ahead of Canada. Already, oil has become the leading industry, with fishing, timber, and tourism taking second, third, and fourth places in Alaskan economy. And the oil potential in Alaska is huge. Offshore wells in Cook Inlet produce natural gas, much of which is processed at plants near Anchorage into nitrate fertilizers. Farther east in the Gulf of Alaska off the town of Cordova there is thought to be another huge reserve of gas and oil, but the most exciting discovery so far has been the

North Slope field, a huge pool between Brooks Range and the Arctic Coast. Near Prudhoe Bay, a well, financed jointly by Humble and Atlantic-Richfield oil companies, brought in the first strike in July of 1968. Estimates of the resource have been growing ever since. The conservative figure puts the pool at 15 billion barrels, but some geologists are convinced it has at least three times as much, maybe even 60 billion barrels. The huge Saudi Arabian and Kuwait fields would take second place in world reserves if the latter estimate were correct.

What do the figures mean in terms of the American consumer? In 1970, the United States used 4.4 billion barrels of oil. By 1980, annual consumption will reach 8 million barrels. Americans need the Alaskan oil.

In Alaska, where more than half the working population today draws pay from the state or federal government, development of new sources of wealth promises a healthier economic foundation. In addition, the Alaskan oil will improve America's position in the balance of world trade, making us less dependent on foreign oil. The taxes and royalties collected each year by the Alaskan government from the North Slope fields would cover the annual state budget twice over. Individual salaries for oil workers on the North Slope would range from $15,000 to $25,000. Many of the workers would be Eskimos and Indians who already live on the North Slope and are used to its winds and its cold.

Oil companies have invested heavily in developing the field. While a well in Texas or Oklahoma can be drilled for $70,000, each North Slope well costs a million dollars. Equipment is freighted north by air. Housing and meals must be provided for workers. Heavy drilling rigs cannot be placed on the tundra without thick foundations of gravel. Even though the drilling rigs are mostly enclosed, the tops must be left open to raise and lower the drill stem and the pipes. Workers sometimes try to drill in a temperature of $-60°$ F. What they do is done slowly. Some workers have estimated it takes twenty-seven times as long to do a job on an Arctic rig as it does in the warmer climates. One man once spent four-and-a-half hours removing eight bolts to change a part on a pump. In Texas, the job would have taken no more than ten minutes.

Work in cold weather requires energy. Merely breathing the cold air expends body heat rapidly. Arctic oil men have already established a reputation as the world's greatest eaters. They need the food for energy.

Barely two years after discovery, however, work in the North Slope oil field came to a virtual halt. Where two thousand men once kept twenty-four drilling rigs busy night and day, the waning months of 1971 found a force of two hundred men with all but two rigs silent. One big problem has caused a delay in development of the huge reserve. How is the oil to be transported to American markets?

We have already seen that the *Manhattan*'s voyage showed the Northwest Passage to be economically unfeasible for a surface tanker, but talk continues on Arctic shipping by submarine. The United States Maritime Administration has atomic-powered submarine tankers of twenty thousand to forty thousand tons under consideration. These could travel the submerged Northwest Passage pioneered by *Seadragon*. General Dynamics Corporation has designed a submarine tanker which could deliver sixty thousand barrels of oil to North Atlantic ports in a round trip of no more than two weeks. Also, submarine tankers and freighters could cross the Arctic Ocean to reach markets of Europe, changing world trade. The present route from Seattle to Oslo, for instance, is a 9,300-mile journey by surface ship. By crossing under the polar ice, a submarine could reduce this to 6,100 miles.

Oil companies, however, want more conventional methods. Seven oil firms, joined as the Alyeska Pipeline Service Company, have asked permission to build a 789-mile oil pipeline to the ice-free port of Valdez in the Gulf of Alaska. The line, forty-eight inches in diameter, would be the largest in the world for crude oil. It would cross three mountain ranges, three earthquake zones, and twenty-three rivers. Originally, cost was estimated at $900 million. Today, the pipeline, if built at all, will cost $2 billion.

Ever since it was proposed, the pipeline has received strong opposition from two local factions. First, the Alaskan natives asked compensation from the gas companies for allowing the line across 641 miles of federal land, land the natives claim is rightfully theirs. Second, environmentalists protested that the line, crossing through the heart of Alaska's wilderness, would do irreparable damage, and a major break in the line would be an ecological disaster. The protests have been so long and loud that both private industry and government have changed their attitudes. The oil companies brought pressure on Congress to settle the long-standing question of native land rights in Alaska. Late in 1971, the Senate and the House hammered out a compromise bill that will grant forty million acres to the native Alaskans. In addition, $962.5 million will be given to regional, native-operated corporations which will expand and improve villages, build schools and hospitals, fund scholarships, and invest in various other projects benefiting the native population. More than half the money is to come from royalties on oils and minerals taken from public lands. The balance—$462.5 million—will come straight from the United States treasury. Though control of the funds and twelve million acres will remain in the hands of the corporations, the per capita value of the grant figures out to $20,000 and 700 acres for each native.

In an attempt to answer protests of environmentalists, the oil companies have made extensive changes in the design of the line. Many of these were at the insistence of the Department of Interior which developed a set of guidelines, an action prompted mainly by conservation pressure from the Friends of the Earth, the Wilderness Society, and the Environmental Defense Fund. Instead of going entirely underground through the tundra as originally planned, the line will be elevated for 48 percent of its length. This is because the crude oil, warmed after passing through pumps, would melt the permafrost and turn the tundra above into a soggy mass that would erode with the first thaw. The oil companies will install monitoring devices along the line that will automatically turn off the flow of oil the moment a leak is detected. Valdez itself will have more safeguards in its harbor loading facilities than any other port of the world. Tankers taking on oil will have floating booms around them to contain any spilled oil. No tanker will be able to pass within a mile of another, thus cutting the risk of collision. Metal connections rather than hoses will be used on all loading pipes. Officials for Alyeska Pipeline Service Company claim $35 million has been spent researching and designing improvements and safeguards. And oil companies have the experience of past mistakes, some their own and some committed by the government.

There is the classic oil-barrel problem at Point Barrow. During early oil exploration in the 1940s, hopeful oilmen shipped 180,000 barrels to Point Barrow. Later, with construction of the DEW line, more barrels arrived. Many were subsequently collected, but some 48,000 abandoned and storm-scattered barrels lie rusting in the tundra today. During winter, ice traps them. In summer, the tundra turns too soggy for men to drive heavy equipment out to collect the barrels. Many barrels were filled with garbage and sewage. This waste and the rusting iron pose serious threat to the water supply at Point Barrow. State and federal officials agree that the barrels must be collected, but the project will cost $1,174,000, an expensive lesson for those who would develop the Arctic.

Mistakes have also taught the oil companies that one does not treat tundra like ordinary soil. You cannot bulldoze it to clear an airstrip or a road. In a single season, the scar becomes a bog and the bog a ditch. Special grasses have been developed to reseed those areas already scarred and special pains are now taken to preserve the permafrost's insulating cover.

The Department of Interior and Congress are expected to approve the pipeline permit by early 1972, but further delay is certain. Court injunctions, won by various conservation groups, promise legal fights at least until 1975.

An alternate route, running the pipe eastward along the Arctic shore to Canada and then south to refineries in the United States is being considered. This would provide a link for Mackenzie Valley oil, and be an all-land route free from the risk of ocean oil spill, but it would also be a loss to Alaskans who would see construction jobs and royalties going to Canada.

Alaska's Governor William Eagan has suggested that the state itself build and operate the controversial pipeline. State ownership, he reasoned, might answer most of the fears of conservationists. In addition, the state could collect $100 million a year from the oil companies using the line.

Some conservation groups, however, have vowed to fight construction of the line no matter who owns and operates it. While the controversy promises to rage for a long time, the very fact that so much attention has centered on the Arctic and its future has to be encouraging. The oil has brought action on the long-delayed problem of native land claims; it has also brought increased concern about the conservation of natural resources and wildlife. It seems today that what action is finally taken will be guided by good sense, better knowledge of the environment, and more concern for future generations. If the pipeline controversy is typical of future Arctic proposals, the wasteful days of Arctic boom and bust are over.

PART TWO

The Antarctic

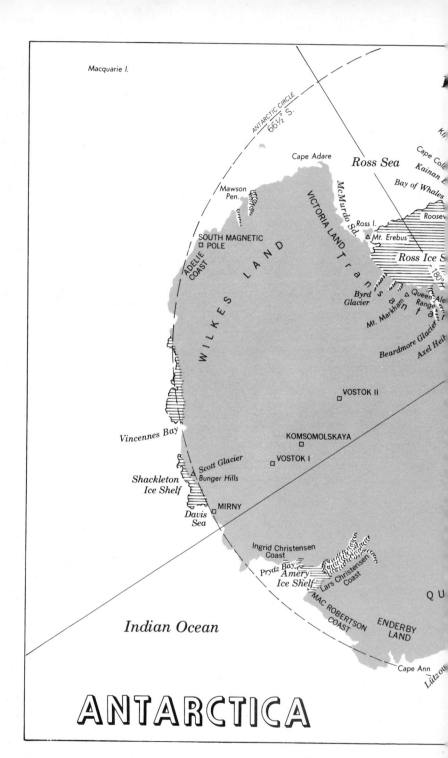

Macquarie I.

ANTARCTIC CIRCLE
66½° S.

Cape Adare   *Ross Sea*

Cape Cole
Kainan L
Bay of Whales

Mawson
Pen.

Roosev

VICTORIA LAND
McMurdo Sd.
Ross I.
△ Mt. Erebus

SOUTH MAGNETIC
POLE

Ross Ice S

ADELIE
COAST

W I L K E S   L A N D

T r a n s

180°

*Byrd
Glacier*
Queen Ale
Range
Mt. Markham

Beardmore Glacier
Axel Heit

VOSTOK II

Vincennes Bay

KOMSOMOLSKAYA

Scott Glacier
VOSTOK I
Bunger Hills

*Shackleton
Ice Shelf*

MIRNY

*Davis
Sea*

Ingrid Christensen
Coast

Prydz Bay
*Amery
Ice Shelf*
Lars Christensen
Coast

MAC ROBERTSON
COAST

ENDERBY
LAND

Q U

Indian Ocean

Cape Ann
Lützo

ANTARCTICA

10

The Greatest Challenge

ENGLAND'S JAMES COOK, sent to locate a southern continent in 1768, was history's first Antarctic explorer. Men had been talking about a southern continent since Greek scholars said a land mass had to be there to keep holding the world upright. Despite two thousand years of discussion and speculation, no one had ever seen this land, and Captain Cook, though he eventually sailed to 71° 10′ south latitude, just off what is now called Marie Byrd Land, also failed to see land.

Discussion of credit for the first sighting of Antarctica still provokes argument. In 1819, forty years after Cook's death,

William Smith, a British merchant skipper, sailed far south of Cape Horn and saw the South Shetland Islands off the Antarctic Peninsula. He reported his discovery to British naval officers at Valparaiso, Chile, and the officers at once saw a chance to control the south side of the important trade passage around Cape Horn. Lieutenant Edward Bransfield sailed beyond the island found by Smith into an open sea and on January 20, 1820, with fog drifting low overhead, a seaman sighted land to the southeast. Bransfield may have come upon Trinity Island off the coast of the peninsula, or he may have found the Antarctic Peninsula itself.

Late the same year, with the beginning of a new sealing season in southern waters, five Yankee ships from Stonington, Connecticut sailed into the sheltered waters of Deception Island and the men established a base. The smallest ship of this fleet was the 45-ton sloop *Hero,* commanded by Nathaniel Palmer, a lad of twenty-one. On November 17, 1820, Palmer was sent south to scout for seal rookeries. He reached an ice-blocked channel between an island and what seemed a continental headland. He continued south, sighting more islands until fog made navigation dangerous. He dropped anchor to wait clearing weather. When the fog lifted, an amazed Palmer found himself between two towering ships of war. Quickly, the young Yankee hoisted the Stars and Stripes. Men on the warships answered by raising flags decorated with the Cross of St. Andrew, emblem of Imperial Russia.

Admiral Fabian Gottlieb von Bellingshausen, in charge of the big ships, was just as startled as Palmer. But the men overcame their surprise, and Palmer soon climbed aboard the Russian flagship to exchange cordial greetings with the admiral. Bellingshausen explained that he was in charge of Russia's first expedition into southern waters. Palmer said he had been hunting seals in the area for several months. With that, the men bid each other goodbye and the ships sailed off in different directions.

The islands Palmer sighted, now called the Palmer Archipelago, are close to the mainland, and it seems very likely that the headland he saw was part of the Antarctic Peninsula. But Bransfield and Bellingshausen might well have seen the mainland first. The question will never be resolved.

While the chance meeting between Russians and Americans was cordial, subsequent meetings between British and American sealers in Antarctic waters were not. During the 1820–21 hunting season, when there were thirty American ships and twenty-two British ships in southern waters, men of the Yankee ship *Huntress* were driven from a rookery by a superior British force, and the British stole eighty skins from the Yankee brig *Charity*.

In the next season, with nearly one hundred British and American ships in the hunt, seal rookeries were virtually wiped out as soon as men discovered them. As seals around the Antarctic Peninsula grew scarce, the search turned eastward. The British became leaders in finding new hunting grounds.

In February of 1823, James Weddell, a British sealing skipper, sailed into open water east of the peninsula and turned back only after reaching 74° 15′ south latitude. The sea which now bears his name is usually clogged with ice, but this was a rare summer, for Weddell saw neither ice nor land. Other ships, sailing under the house flag of the Enderby Brothers of London, pressed farther and farther east, skirting the continental shore and eventually reaching a promontory facing the heart of the Indian Ocean, a region now called Enderby Land.

Antarctic sealing declined before the last century was half over. Hazards were too great, seals too few. The next men to come south sailed for science.

James Clark Ross's discovery of the North Magnetic Pole on Boothia Peninsula in 1831 had explained much about magnetic variation. The British explorer next hoped to locate the South Magnetic Pole, but in 1840, before Ross could complete preparations, a French expedition under Jules Sébastien César Dumont d'Urville sailed from a base on Tasmania. Dumont d'Urville at first was interested in general exploration, but when he found himself in Antarctic waters ahead of Ross, he decided to see how close he could sail to the magnetic pole. Following the compass, he made a landfall on January 19, 1840, almost due south of Tasmania. His compass needle was four degrees from vertical position, telling him that the pole he sought lay many miles inland. The Frenchman landed on a small, off-shore island and made a claim for his king. Dumont d'Urville called his discovery Adelie Land in honor of his wife. (By strange coincidence, the South Magnetic Pole, which for some unknown reason migrates some eight miles to the northwest each year, reached the coast in 1965 at 140° west longitude, almost the precise position of the French landfall. Dumont d'Urville, sailing carefully off the berg-cluttered coast, was startled a week after his landfall to see a strange ship approach through the fog. She was *Porpoise,* one of the ships of the long-planned and much-delayed Antarctic expedition of the United States.

The American sailors, under command of Navy Lieutenant Charles Wilkes, had also beaten Ross to the Antarctic.
Proposed in 1826 by sealers wanting better charts, the expedition was delayed by an economy-minded Congress until the
sealing era was well past. When appropriations finally came,
they did not provide for adequate ships or equipment and
the force of 440 men had clothing more suited for the sub-
tropics. All six of the expedition's ships were old, some had
rotten planking. *Sea Gull,* a small pilot boat, sank with all
hands off Cape Horn soon after the Americans met their
first serious storm. On January 12, 1840, when Wilkes
reached pack ice in the sloop-of-war *Vincennes,* he was all
alone. The other ships trailed somewhere in his wake. The
sloop *Peacock* and the brig *Porpoise* soon caught up, however, and the three ships began working through the pack.
On January 19, lookouts sighted land, but their position as
later charts showed was 165 miles from any land and about
400 miles east of the French landfall. The men may have
seen a mirage. Subsequently Wilkes made frequent real
landfalls as the ships worked westward.

Wilkes's men suffered from cold and complained bitterly.
Officers had difficulty keeping discipline. Just beyond 100°
west longitude, a huge tongue of ice, now known as the
Shackleton Ice Shelf, forced Wilkes away from land. His
frostbitten, exhausted men were close to mutiny. Wilkes
decided to sail for New Zealand. He had skirted nearly 1,600
miles of continental coast, and at New Zealand the rest of
his ships and men were accounted for, but Wilkes was not
to receive acclaim. His officers, signing charges of injustice
and oppression, forced a court martial. Wilkes told the court
stern leadership had helped bring his men through the

ordeal. He was eventually acquitted, but the trial deadened America's Antarctic zeal.

Ross sailed from England in 1841, a year after Wilkes and Dumont d'Urville. The Scotsman hoped that by going east of their landfalls he could find passage that would allow him to sail his two ships, *Erebus* and *Terror,* to the magnetic pole. This led him to the most significant Antarctic discovery yet. Ross sailed through the pack into an ice-free sea, and came upon a headland where the coast turned sharply to the south, a landfall he called Cape Adare. He continued south, keeping the high land on his right in view, searching constantly for a passage that might lead him to the magnetic pole, but the rocky coast stretched on without interruption. At one point, Ross landed on an island and made claim for England. He called the region Victoria Land for his queen.

It soon became obvious there was no way to sail to the goal he sought, but this ice-free sea intrigued Ross. He and his men became the first to sail below 75° south latitude, and still they continued, looking constantly for ice, but it was a huge peak, belching smoke and fire that first loomed above the southern horizon. Sailing closer, Ross could see two tall mountains, one a dormant volcano and the other active. At their base to the east, high cliffs of ice stretched away in the distance. At the right the ice cliffs were indented by a bay. Ross named the peaks Erebus and Terror in honor of his ships. Mount Erebus has since been found to be 12,450 feet high, the only known active volcano in the southern continent and among the world's tallest. The land from which both peaks rose has since been named Ross Island and the sea Ross Sea. Ross called the inlet west of the peaks McMurdo Bay, a name since changed to McMurdo Sound. The white cliffs to the east proved to be the front edge of a 700-foot-thick ice blanket with an area larger than France. It is now called the Ross Ice Shelf. It proved to be the highway for the first expeditions to the interior of the continent.

Ross sailed east along cliffs, hoping to find more open water leading south, but drifting sea ice eventually forced him to turn away. He returned to winter base in Tasmania, but the next season brought him back, picking up where he left off. He reached another inlet, one since named the Bay of Whales, and he managed to sail to 79° 9′ south latitude. Then once again, it was time to retreat.

On his return to England, Ross received deserved acclaim, but interest in polar exploration had focused on the Arctic. Ross joined the futile search for Franklin and never again returned to Antarctica.

Antarctic interest did not revive until 1895 when the Sixth International Geographical Congress, meeting in London, concluded that "the explorations of the Antarctic regions is the greatest piece of geographical exploration still to be undertaken."[13] The words challenged bold men.

A Belgian expedition under Adrien de Gerlache sailed south in 1897 and earned the distinction of being first to spend a winter below the Antarctic Circle. It was not planned. Ice trapped the ship west of the Antarctic Peninsula, and all men might have perished if the first mate had not shot seal and the ship's doctor insisted that the men eat the fresh meat. The mate was Norway's Amundsen. The doctor was Frederick Cook of the United States.

The twentieth century opened with three separate expeditions to the southern continent. Germany's Erich von Drygalski landed on the coast just west of the ice shelf that had stopped Wilkes. Ice trapped his ship, but by spreading ashes from a nearby volcano, the Germans increased absorption of the sun's heat, thus hastening the thaw and escaping before supplies gave out.

Meanwhile, a Swedish expedition, which had landed on the Antarctic Peninsula, was marooned for two winters after ice blocked and later crushed the party's ship. The men, led by Otto Nordenskjöld, nephew of the man who conquered the Northeast Passage, lived on seal and penguin meat and fish they caught with hooks fashioned from belt buckles. An Argentine vessel, sent by an English explorer, rescued the Swedes. The Englishman was Ernest Shackleton who had just escaped another dangerous Antarctic venture.

Shackleton served under Robert Falcon Scott, an English naval officer, who led his expedition to the Ross Ice Shelf early in 1902. At the eastern limit of the shelf, Scott discovered King Edward VII Land, now known to be a peninsula. At Bay of Whales, Scott rose eight hundred feet above the ice in a captive balloon for the first aerial inspection of the ice shelf. It stretched southward in an unbroken plain. At McMurdo Sound, Scott and his thirty-seven seamen and scientists established base. They built a house on the southwest tip of Ross Island and stocked it with provisions for the winter.

The men kept busy through the long night making plans and preparing for excursions in the coming summer. Scott's major undertaking was to march south, find out how far inland the massive ice shelf extended, and if possible, reach the South Pole. A second sledge party, under Lieutenant Albert B. Armitage, would explore the high mountains rising to the west of McMurdo Sound. Preliminary depot laying began with the first light in October, and on November 2, 1902, the southern march began. With Scott were Shackleton and Dr. Edward A. Wilson, who served both as expedition doctor and artist.

The men soon found they had not brought enough dogs. Clinging snow slowed the sledges as both men and dogs struggled to haul supplies south. Wilson suffered snowblindness from the sunlight reflected off the ice. Under protection, his eyes eventually improved, but all three men grew terribly weak, especially Shackleton. Then their dogs began to die from some unknown malady. At 82° 17′ south latitude, 350 miles out of McMurdo, Scott decided to turn home. With all dogs dead, it was necessary to man-haul the sledges. Shackleton eventually collapsed and had to be hauled himself, but fortunately they had a following wind and tent floors to rig as sails. The wind brought them home, and Shackleton, who was suffering from scurvy, was carried aboard a relief vessel and sent home.

Though Scott had hoped to travel farther, the journey had greatly extended knowledge of the Ross Ice Shelf and the Transantarctic Mountains on the shelf's western border.

Armitage meanwhile had led his party onto the plateau to the west of McMurdo Sound and reached an elevation of nine thousand feet before turning back. In the final season, the summer of 1903–04, Scott led a party west and marched two hundred miles beyond Armitage's turning point. The men returned to base through an ice-free valley filled with the cheerful sound of running water. Algae, thick as peat, grew in stagnant pools. The men were startled to find the body of a Weddell seal. No one could imagine what had caused the animal to stray so far from the sea.

In England, Scott's three seasons in the Antarctic were hailed as a huge success, and deservedly so. No single group had yet brought home such a huge collection of new information about the continent, and no one had gone so far south. Talk began almost at once of a second Scott expedition that would reach the pole, but the next group of Englishmen to sail for the Ross Sea was led not by Scott but by Shackleton.

Without the formal backing of the Royal Geographic Society that Scott enjoyed, Shackleton had tremendous difficulty in raising funds, but he was a stubborn and persuasive man, and he was motivated in part by a desire to vindicate himself for the weakness that almost brought disaster to the first southern march.

Nimrod, a forty-four-year-old Norwegian sealer, very small for an Antarctic expedition, sailed from London on July 30, 1907. The ship carried such a load that her rail stood just three-and-a-half feet from the water. Though his ship was small, Shackleton's plans were big. He would try for both the geographic and the magnetic poles. He would rely on Manchurian ponies and a motorized sledge for transport, and he would do his work in two summers.

Shackleton and his men built their base on Ross Island not far from Scott's house. As before, the first summer was spent unloading gear, building shelter, training men, and testing equipment. The motor sledge bogged down in soft snow. It helped in unloading the ship, but it obviously would not serve in a long march.

Work at the base progressed fast enough the first season to permit one excursion. Australian geology professor T. W. Edgeworth David and five other men climbed to the smoking top of Mount Erebus.

Under his plan for the next season, Shackleton and four others would make the southern march while David with two companions would try for the magnetic pole which lay somewhere to the northwest beyond the mountains.

Shackleton's biggest worry was transport. One pony had died aboard ship, three had died from eating sand, and another died from eating shavings from a chemically treated piece of wood. Only four animals were left to establish depots and support the southern march. Though he realized he was severely limited, Shackleton and his men started out on November 8, 1908.

It took four weeks of hard marching to reach the point where he, Wilson, and Scott had turned back five years before. Beyond that point, killing of ponies began. It was part of the plan. As loads diminished there was no need for them, and without adequate fodder, the extra animals would starve. When the men finally stood at the base of the Transantarctic Mountains, just one pony remained.

From a small peak the men searched the barrier for a way up. They saw a huge glacier extending up through the cliffs like an inviting highway. Shackleton named it Beardmore Glacier. Subsequent surveys showed it to be fifteen miles wide and one hundred miles long. It was no easy highway for the five weary man.

Soon after starting up, the pony, with half the party's meat supply, vanished down a crevasse. The men also fell through thin crusts of snow into crevasses, but each time were saved from death by the hauling harness tied to the loaded sledges behind. All men, however, suffered bruises. Their rate of march dropped almost to a crawl, but rations, already diminished by the loss of the pony's pack, continued to be consumed at the same rate.

On Christmas Eve, the party reached the top of the glacier and gazed upon a dazzling plain of ice. They stood 9,095 feet above the sea, gasping for breath in the thin air. A cold wind stung their faces, and each man nursed bruised and aching muscles, but they could not turn back. The South Pole lay just three hundred miles ahead.

They trudged southward. Each hour Shackleton stopped them for a brief rest. Then they leaned into their hauling harnesses again and trudged on. At the end of each day's march, they put up their tents, ate a warm meal, and slept, but neither the rests nor the sleep adequately restored their ebbing strength. January 9, 1909, just 112 miles from the pole, Shackleton reluctantly decided they must turn back if they were to save themselves.

The return march tested the five men to the limit of strength and courage. Again, a trailing wind and sledge sails made the difference, but the threat of starvation followed all the way.

During the southern march, David, Dr. A. F. Mackay, and Douglas Mawson, who would become Australia's leading Arctic explorer, located the South Magnetic Pole at 155° 16′ east longitude and 72° 25′ south latitude. It was January 16, 1909, when the first men to stand at this spot raised the Union Jack and took possession in the name of England's King Edward VII. The men then gave three loud cheers. The party shortened the return to base by a rendezvous with *Nimrod* on the Scott Coast north of McMurdo Sound.

On March 4, 1909, with all members of the expedition safely aboard, the *Nimrod* sailed for home.

11

The Age of Heroes

NOT LONG AFTER Shackleton's return, Scott announced plans for a second expedition. Though there would be considerable scientific work, the main undertaking would be a march to the pole. English confidence soared. It was laughable to suggest that any other nation might win the prize.

Norway's Roald Amundsen gave no thought to an Antarctic venture until a day in the spring of 1909, the day America's Robert Peary returned from the Arctic to announce that he had reached the North Pole. The news shattered Amundsen's life-long dream, and forced him to reconsider immediate plans. He had always wanted to be first at the North Pole. He was about to launch an assault upon it when Peary announced victory.

Now Amundsen knew he must change his plans. He sailed for Antarctica.

The Scott and Amundsen expeditions differed greatly. Scott would land fifty-five men on the continent and rely mostly on Manchurian ponies for transport. Amundsen would land nine men and rely entirely on dogs. Early in 1911, both parties were established, making preparations for the winter and the march south that would begin as early in the southern spring as possible. Scott's camp was at McMurdo Sound. Amundsen's stood to the east at Bay of Whales. Not only was the Norwegian camp eighty-seven miles closer to the pole than the English camp, but the weather on the east side of the Ross Ice Shelf was far better than the weather to the west. This enabled Amundsen and his four trail companions to start south on October 19, 1911, fifteen days ahead of Scott.

The greatest difficulty for the Norwegians came in the crevassed region of Axel Heiberg Glacier, the acclivity they chose to reach the Antarctic Plateau. They were forced to work through the dangerous region in a blizzard, but the weather soon cleared again. Amundsen and his men arrived at the South Pole on December 14. They rested there four days before starting back to the Bay of Whales. Weather on the day they left the pole was almost balmy by Antarctic standards. The thermometer showed $-2.2°$ F and there was no more than a slight breeze. The five men arrived at their base on January 25, 1912. They had covered the 1,860 miles to the pole and back in ninety-nine days.

Scott started south with eleven others on November 3, 1911, planning to send some men back as supply depots were established along the route. Just Scott and four others would make the march to the pole. By the time the Englishmen started up the broken surface of Beardmore Glacier they were man-hauling sledges. Though the few dogs Scott brought had performed well, he sent them home with a support team. Scott could not forget how dogs had disappointed him on his first southern march. The ponies, useless in the crevassed ice of Beardmore were all shot prior to the ascent.

Soon after reaching the plateau, Scott sent the last of the support crew home. That was on January 3, 1912. Five days later, a blizzard stopped the southern march. When the weather cleared, ice crystals dragged at the sledge runners like gravel. The men were bruised, frostbitten, and close to exhaustion. They may have been suffering from malnutrition. On January 16, they made a discovery that almost broke their spirits. An empty sledge, left on the trail by the Norwegians, made it clear that the Englishmen had lost the race to the South Pole, but they pressed on. Next day they reached the goal. It was marked by an empty tent and a Norwegian flag.

Scott and his men, extremely tired and deeply discouraged, turned for home. They never made it. Edgar "Taff" Evans died of injuries received in a fall near the base of Beardmore Glacier. Laurence E. G. Oates, crippled by frostbitten hands and feet, ended his suffering by walking away from camp into a blizzard. Scott, his old companion Dr. Wilson, and Henry R. Bowers struggled on, but they grew so weak that they could travel only a few miles a day. Food gave out. A blizzard stopped them and held them in their tent. They died there of cold and starvation just eleven miles short of a major food depot.

England mourned. National pride suffered. When Amundsen came to England to lecture on his Antarctic conquest he faced criticism and insult. Some Englishmen illogically blamed the Norwegian for the tragedy. Amundsen thought it was all a poor show of sportsmanship. He did not fully understand the English pride.

That pride suffered further from the knowledge that an ambitious German expedition might wrest another victory in the field England had so long dominated. Wilhelm Filchner, a geophysicist, had established an Antarctic base while Scott and Amundsen were on the polar trail. Filchner and his men planned to march from the coast of the Weddell Sea to the Ross Sea, crossing the continent by way of the pole. Unfortunately for the Germans, their camp was destroyed when a berg broke from the ice shelf that now bears Filchner's name. Plans for the march were abandoned.

Soon after this, as if responding to his country's need for renewed pride, Shackleton announced that he would lead a march across the continent. There would be two parties. The main group would head for the pole from the Weddell Sea just as Filchner had planned. A second, support party would march inland from McMurdo Sound, establishing supply depots across the Ross Ice Shelf. The depots would serve the main group on the final leg of its march.

Fund-raising efforts delayed the start of the Imperial Trans-Antarctic Expedition until 1914, and then the project was almost scrapped due to the start of World War I. Many of Shackleton's men felt duty-bound to fight, but Winston Churchill, then First Lord of the Admiralty, encouraged the expedition to proceed. With the best wishes of their country behind them, the men sailed south in *Endurance,* a stout ship built especially for polar ice.

The men never set foot on the Southern Continent. Ice trapped the ship in the Weddell Sea and carried her in a slow, clockwise drift that led slowly toward open water near the northern tip of the Antarctic Peninsula. For several months, the ship seemed safe, but then pressure began. Stout frames groaned and cracked. On October 17, 1915, Shackleton told his men to abandon her. They took off the three ship's boats and all the stores they could handle. Five weeks later, the ship sank.

Twenty-eight men, with limited stores and no way to call for rescue, stood on the ice and watched *Endurance* go down. Their situation seemed hopeless to some, but in Shackleton the men had a determined leader who would not admit defeat. He started them marching across the ice, working in relays to haul the boats and supplies toward the shore of the peninsula three hundred miles to the west. The task proved impossible. The weight of the boats was too great, the ice too fractured and uneven. The men had to wait for the drift of the pack to carry them to the open sea. They lived on seals and penguins, eating the meat and using the blubber for fuel.

By his own fortitude and steady confidence, Shackleton set an example for all during the long wait for freedom. When the ice about them began to crack and toss on the surge of sea waves, the men prepared the boats. They launched them in a lead of rough water on April 9, 1916. The men had been prisoners of the ice nearly fifteen months, but their worst ordeal lay ahead.

They tried to row for nearby islands in the South Shetland group, but currents and wind worked against them. When they stopped to rest on a drifting floe, the ice cracked, forcing them to scramble back to the boats. Then a storm carried them away from land. Soaked by water that froze on their clothing, tortured by thirst, hunger, and fatigue, the men bailed and rowed for their lives. They weathered the storm. Then, with favorable drift and hard rowing, they made landfall at bleak, ice-bound Elephant Island. A wind-swept bar of gravel offered the only safe landing, but the men welcomed the shore gladly. Six days in open boats during the approach of Antarctic winter was enough for even the hardiest sailors, but Shackleton knew he could not rest long if he were to save his men. He had the ship's carpenter strip planks from one of the boats to build a deck on another.

He chose five men to go with him, and on April 24, with what stores could be spared and a pitifully small supply of drinking water, he set sail for South Georgia Island 870 miles to the northeast across the world's roughest ocean. His boat was twenty-two and a half feet long. Ice had to be chopped from the rigging and deck again and again to keep its weight from capsizing the boat. Huge waves gathered behind her and swept the deck. The men had to bail quickly before the next wave came up to swamp them.

South Georgia was the only outpost of civilization Shackleton could reach. The unhandy boat could never have sailed close enough to the wind to reach Cape Horn. If he missed South Georgia, Shackleton knew the next landfall would be Africa. His navigation had to be perfect. It was. He beached the boat through surf on the west side of the island on May 10, 1916, seventeen days after leaving Elephant Island. Unfortunately, a broken rudder made the boat useless, and all the settlements were on the east side of the mountainous island. Shackleton had no choice but to climb over the steep ridge of ice and rock to the settlements. No one had attempted such a feat. Residents of South Georgia thought it impossible.

He left three men with the boat and took two others with him. Part of their hike over the mountains was in the dark. Once they sat on a coiled rope and slid several hundred feet down an icy escarpment. Near the end, they lowered themselves by rope through a waterfall, but they finally made it. At the whaling station, men who had met Shackleton two years earlier did not recognize him, but he quickly made his needs known. A whale catcher picked up the men on the opposite side of the island within hours. Rescue of the men on Elephant Island took longer, as ice blocked the relief ship for several weeks, but finally all men left on Elephant Island were recovered. The only serious casualty among them was one man's loss of toes due to frostbite.

Shackleton's heroic saga provided a fitting end to the Antarctic's age of heroes, an age that put man's strength and courage to test against nature's greatest challenge.

12

The Modern Age

THE SHACKLETON EXPEDITION did not escape tragedy. Of the ten men sent to McMurdo Sound, three died of scurvy during the futile depot-laying march. Had there been radio communication, the march and the deaths could have been avoided.

Douglas Mawson, one of David's companions in the conquest of the South Magnetic Pole, headed his own expedition to the Adelie Coast in 1912 and became the first to make successful use of radio in the Antarctic. By relaying signals through Macquarie Island, Mawson communicated with friends in Australia.

Mawson's expedition also brought the first airplane to the Antarctic. The plane, a single-wing Vickers, had one major fault. It could not fly. During his drive for funds, Mawson had barnstormed Australia with the plane and cracked it up. He landed it on Antarctica just the same, and with wings removed, the plane served as a sledge hauler.

First to actually fly over the Antarctic was George Hubert Wilkins, the veteran Arctic explorer. Wilkins, using a base at Deception Island, made several flights above the Antarctic Peninsula during the southern summer of 1928-29. He mistakenly reported that the peninsula was a group of islands separated by ice-clogged channels. The error pointed up a persistent problem in aerial survey: ground parties are needed to fix key landmarks before photos and observations from the air can be effective.

While Wilkins made his pioneer flights, an American expedition, the first since Wilkes's troubled voyage, headed south. Commander (later Admiral) Richard E. Byrd hoped to test the full potential of aircraft in Antarctic exploration. In pursuing this hope, Byrd brought the modern age to the southern continent. The age involved more than new machines and technology. It involved a change in attitude that paralleled Byrd's own maturing goals. Instead of heroic feats, fame, and headlines, the modern age would seek knowledge.

Byrd had already won the fame because of his North Pole flight and a flight in 1927 across the Atlantic with three companions. His fame helped him raise $800,000 in private donations for the Antarctic venture, but so did his friendship with two leading financiers—John D. Rockefeller, Jr. and Edsel Ford.

Byrd purchased two ships, *City of New York,* a wooden-hulled sailing vessel, and *Eleanor Bolling,* a steel-hulled freighter. In addition, he bought three monoplanes, a Fokker, a Fairchild, and a large Ford. The Ford, with three engines, would be used for an assault on the South Pole.

Byrd picked the Bay of Whales for his port and established a base of three buildings with connecting tunnels not far from Amundsen's camp of seventeen years before. The men worked hard to put up plane hangars, dog kennels, and three radio towers before winter closed in on them. The biggest undertaking of the season, however, was the unloading of 655 tons of supplies. Byrd figured later that dogs and men traveled a total of twelve thousand miles in the many cargo trips between the ships and the base. But the work went well, and the Antarctic outpost soon took shape. Byrd called it Little America.

The first flight was made in the Fairchild on January 15, 1929, just three weeks after the expedition landed. Twelve days after the test flight, Byrd made an exploratory sweep in the Fairchild along the ice cliffs east over King Edward VII Peninsula to Scott's Nunataks, these being the only peaks positioned accurately on charts of the region. Byrd sighted several other peaks to the east as well as a large bay beyond the peninsula before fog forced him to turn south. He came upon fourteen large peaks and named them the Rockefeller Mountains, his first important discovery.

Three weeks later, Byrd took off again and flew 130 miles east of Little America, beyond the Rockefeller Mountains to a peak resembling the Matterhorn of Switzerland. LaGorce Peak, as it is known today, stands 2,700 feet above sea level and is the highest peak of the King Edward VII Peninsula.

These discoveries made geologist Laurence M. Gould,

Byrd's second in command, extremely anxious to begin wielding his rock hammer. On March 7, the Fokker flew a small survey party under Gould's command to the base of the Rockefeller Mountains. For a week, the men kept in touch daily with Little America by radio. Then the signals stopped. Byrd flew east in the Fairchild as soon as weather permitted. He found Gould's camp and landed to discover the Fokker a total wreck. Gould and his men told how winds roaring up to 150 miles an hour had lifted the Fokker from its moorings and slammed it down on the ice several hundred yards away from camp, destroying the radio as well as the plane.

Two trips were necessary to take all the men back to base, and while Byrd was awaiting the return of the Fairchild, he conversed with friends in the United States. A field radio carried his messages to Little America, which relayed them to New York. This indeed was a new age in exploration.

The rescue flights were the last of the season. Forty-four men settled in for the winter at Little America. Dogs had to be tended, weather records maintained, and planes and shelters had to be checked regularly. Any extra time was devoted to planning and preparation for the next season.

Gould, with the aid of a support party, would lead a survey south by dog sledge to inspect and map as much of the Queen Maud Mountains as possible. The geological party, as it was called, could also serve for ground rescue if the Ford were forced down on the polar flight. Gould and his dog drivers and Byrd and his pilots went over supply lists again and again, seeking ways to save weight. The pilots decided to lay a fuel depot for the Ford's return by a preliminary flight on the ice shelf at the base of the mountains.

Byrd let his sledge teams start south first. Then on November 18, 1929, with all three motors roaring, the Ford took off from the ice shelf at Little America and turned south. The decision on a depot-laying flight proved fortunate because the plane's fuel consumption was much higher than expected. All went well in the landing and take-off from the ice at the base of the Queen Maud Range, but on the return, one hundred miles from Little America, the engines died. Pilot Harold June set the big craft down on the ice without damage, and a call for help went out by radio. Shortly, the Fairchild set down beside the Ford, and the big plane's tanks were replenished.

Back at Little America, mechanics reduced the size of the air intakes on the Ford's carburetors to reduce fuel consumption. It was a risky alteration, particularly without a test flight. The plane might not be able to climb as high as before, but on November 25, when Gould radioed from the base of the mountains that the weather was clear, Byrd did not hesitate. The flight for the pole began. Norwegian Bernt Balchen flew the plane. June operated the radio. Ashley C. McKinley had charge of the aerial camera. Byrd was navigator as well as flight commander.

The engines pulled well even after Balchen began climbing to clear the mountains. The real test for the changed carburetors would come when the craft neared its ceiling of eleven thousand feet, a limit that left little margin for clearing the passes.

Byrd decided to use Liv Glacier for the ascent. Amundsen had climbed Axel Heiberg Glacier just to the east, but it seemed dangerously narrow. Liv, at least at the base, was broad, with plenty of room between the cliffs for the plane to turn back in case of trouble.

At first, the plane passed above a smooth river of ice, but ten miles south big cracks appeared. The air above became turbulent. The plane plunged and tossed. The rate of climb slowed dangerously. The pass narrowed and soon tall, stark cliffs of rock rose close on either side. Byrd sighted over the nose of the plane at the crest of the glacier. One moment the ship pointed at sky, the next moment ice. Balchen began gesturing and trying to yell above the roar of the straining engines. No one caught his words, but all understood. They must jettison cargo.

Byrd had a tough decision to make, with little time to make it. If he dumped emergency food, he and his companions would be in peril if the ship were forced down. If he dumped fuel, it would mean turning back short of the pole. Byrd knew his companions. They had come on this expedition for one purpose. McKinley, in fact, had already shoved a food pack toward the trap door of the fuselage. Byrd ordered it dumped. That helped, but not enough. As air turbulence increased, Balchen called out again. The second and last food pack plunged to the ice. The plane rose just in time to clear the crest. The most dramatic and the riskiest moment of the flight was over. Byrd would not expose his men to such a risk again.

Beyond the glacier, the landscape below became a monotonous plain of white. It continued that way to the pole. As the plane used up fuel and lightened, Balchen managed to climb fifteen hundred feet above the ice, but even at that height, nothing appeared on the horizon to break the monotony.

At the South Pole, Byrd dropped a United States Flag weighted with a stone taken from the grave of Floyd Bennett, companion on the North Pole flight (Bennett had died from pneumonia contracted on an Arctic rescue flight in 1928).

The return to Little America was made without difficulty. The Ford's skis touched down nineteen hours after take-off. The polar flight, longest yet made in Antarctica, did not give Byrd the satisfaction he had expected. It actually revealed little not already known. More inviting territory lay eastward, beyond 150° west longitude. It was a territory bigger than Alaska, unclaimed and unknown. Byrd called it Marie Byrd Land in honor of his wife. A week after the polar flight, he flew east.

Byrd found a new group of mountains, running north and south one hundred and eighty miles with peaks five thousand feet high. He named them for Edsel Ford. At the western base of these ranges were patches of open water which later proved to be part of a large inlet. Sulzberger Bay, Byrd called it, honoring another sponsor, the publisher of The New York *Times.*

Meanwhile, Gould's sledging party, which would cover fifteen hundred miles in eleven weeks, found the base of the Queen Maud Mountains to be composed of the most ancient rock known to geologists—three billion years old. Upper levels, however, were horizontal layers of sandstone formed much more recently. The mountain formation was a horst—massive blocks thrust up without great tipping or folding of the strata—undoubtedly an extension of the range examined by the Scott and Shackleton expeditions near McMurdo Sound. The geological party, too, crossed the 150th meridian before returning to Little America.

Gould's return brought the expedition's work of discovery to a close. As the winter of 1930 descended, *City of New York,* after fighting through ice and headwinds, arrived to take the men home.

Byrd knew he must return to Antarctica. But organizing and raising funds for a second expedition took months of hard work. In America and Europe prosperity had given way to depression. Cash donations were rare. Firms preferred to donate products. Institutions loaned equipment but withheld grants. Byrd, however, persisted, and late in 1933 headed a second expedition south.

This time he had four planes, including an autogyro, forerunner of the helicopter, and a Curtiss-Wright Condor with a range of 1,300 miles. He also brought 153 sledge dogs, a snow tractor, and three trucks fitted with tracks donated by French automaker André Citroen. These trucks proved a success and became the first motor vehicles used for extended Antarctic travel.

At Little America, the men found the three buildings sagging under accumulated snow but still usable. Eight new buildings went up beside them. During this construction, Byrd made two attempts to sail his ship eastward along the coast of Marie Byrd Land, but ice stopped him each time. He landed at Little America to direct preparations for the winter and take control of a special project.

Instead of collecting weather data from just one station, Byrd planned an advance base on the ice sheet. At one time, he thought of establishing this base on the plateau beyond the Queen Maud Range, but it was already far too late in the season for such an undertaking. As it turned out, the advance base was established 123 miles south of Little America, and because of transportation problems, the three-man staff

Byrd hoped to leave there had to be cut. He did not want to leave two men alone in the Antarctic night. Isolation did strange things to even the closest friendships. Byrd also was reluctant to ask any man to winter alone. He found the solution by selecting himself.

Byrd had confidence in his organization and his men. He knew Little America could get through the winter without him. Besides, he was curious to test the effects of winter isolation; and the fact that no man had done such a thing before appealed to Byrd.

Construction of Advance Base was simple. Men dug a trench in the ice, lowered a box-like cabin into the cavity, and covered it with snow. The only things showing above the surface were weather instruments and a stovepipe. Caves in the ice beside Byrd's cabin housed food and fuel and a gasoline-powered generator to provide electricity for the radio. On March 28, 1934, Byrd watched the construction party disappear over the northern horizon. Then he lowered himself through the trapdoor into his snug cabin. Outside temperature soon dropped to −60° F. Inside, he remained comfortable. He had a well-stocked library, his diary, and the daily radio contact with Little America to keep him from boredom. It did not seem a bad life, not at first, but in the sixth week of isolation, Byrd decided something had gone wrong.

Words blurred before his eyes when he tried to read. He had a headache, felt depressed, irritated. Could it be the oil stove? He plugged seams in the stovepipe and made sure the vent outside was clear of snow. He felt better. Fumes from the stove, however, were not the only poisons in the air. The gasoline generator was far more dangerous.

On May 31, while Byrd tapped out his message to Little America, the engine began to miss. He found the engine chamber thick with smoke, but he stepped in just the same to adjust the carburetor. The fumes knocked him out. He regained consciousness on his knees. He crawled back to his cabin, turned off the radio, and fell onto his bunk. The generator continued to run. Byrd knew he must turn it off, but for a long time he could not muster the strength to rise. Finally, however, he staggered to the engine chamber and silenced the motor.

Byrd never regained full health through the rest of the winter. For several days, he could not hold down any food, but his great fear was that his companions at Little America would learn of his plight and try to come to his rescue, which would be far too risky in the dead of winter. Once, with the thermometer showing $-80°$ F, Byrd could not breathe outside without shielding his face. A trail party would have no chance in such cold.

For weeks he managed to hide his condition. He was not an expert at Morse code. His transmission was normally slow, but he had to stop often to gather strength.

At Little America, Thomas Poulter, second in command of this second expedition, wanted to determine the height of aurora displays. By simultaneous obesrvations at two points he could figure altitude by triangulation. Poulter told Byrd he wanted to join him at Advance Base before winter ended to carry out the project. Byrd saw this as a chance for relief without risk. He told Poulter to come, but to pick his weather and take no chances.

The weather, however, delayed Poulter's start, and radiomen at Little America began to suspect that something more than inexperience was causing Byrd's erratic transmissions. By the time Poulter and two others started south on August 8, all were alarmed. Poulter's suspicions, however, had not prepared him for the appearance of his leader. Poulter gazed at an emaciated, hollow-cheeked man. Even Byrd's voice had a husky, unnatural sound. Poulter and his companions moved in with Byrd and helped him regain his health. In October, a plane picked the leader up and returned him to Little America. Poulter gathered up the records collected at Advance Base. He noted with quiet pride that the weather observations were complete. Byrd, despite all, had not missed a day.

Sledge parties were already in the field when Byrd returned. A southern party led by Quin Blackburn climbed through the Queen Maud Mountains by way of Scott Glacier, surveying as they went. The glacier, one hundred and twenty miles long, took ten days of hard marching. The men found several seams of coal, and collected plant fossils from the sandstone cliffs, and were startled to find many varieties of lichens growing on the northern faces of rocks, at 86° south latitude. These remain today the most southern evidence of plant life found in the world.

A seismic party marched east into Marie Byrd Land and found, by touching off explosions and measuring echo travel time, that the ice ranged from one thousand to two thousand feet thick. Just south of Little America, other seismic shots revealed an island beneath the ice shelf. This rise, called Roosevelt Island, split the outward flowing ice and created the Bay of Whales.

Paul Siple, heading another eastern sledge party, reached the northern end of the Edsel Ford Ranges for the farthest surface penetration yet into Marie Byrd Land. Siple, who had been a Boy Scout on Byrd's first expedition, found that the mountains were of different rock from those of the Antarctic Peninsula. Siple and his men also collected lichens and ice stained with colonies of microscopic animals.

The season of flight from Little America extended discovery east and south. One aim was to determine whether a strait linked the Weddell and Ross seas. It seemed to the fliers that a distinct coastal rise marked the eastern side of the Ross Ice Shelf and that a strait was unlikely.

In other eastern flights, more peaks beyond the Edsel Ford Ranges appeared, and the southern flights revealed that the Queen Maud Range extended farther east than suspected. Such discoveries were tantalizing for Byrd and his men. The southern summer ended far too soon. It was difficult to abandon Little America once again when so much work remained to be done, but the expedition was not equipped for another winter.

Less than a year after Byrd and his men left Little America, two men walked in from the south and used the abandoned base for shelter. They were Herbert Hollick-Kenyon, a Canadian pilot, and Lincoln Ellsworth, an American explorer. Their plane had run out of gas twelve miles from Little America, ending history's first trans-Antarctic flight.

Ellsworth, heir to a fortune which had helped finance Amundsen's Arctic flights, had become interested in the southern continent while attending a memorial service for Scott and his companions in 1913. The American flier studied all he could find about Antarctic weather and decided it was too unpredictable for conventional flying. Instead of waiting for favorable predictions before taking off, Ellsworth thought it would be better to follow good weather while it lasted, then land and wait out whatever storms might come. Rather than depend on a weatherman, he would put his faith in his machine. On Ellsworth's orders, Northrop Airplane Company designed a low-winged monoplane with a 600-horsepower Wasp engine and ski landing gear. This was one of the first planes equipped with wing flaps for slow landing speed. Its powerful engine could lift it from a short runway.

Ellsworth headed south in 1933. He made successful test flights from the Bay of Whales, but his plane was damaged by cracking ice and the venture had to be canceled for the season. He went south again in 1934, but bad weather frustrated him. In 1935, with Wilkins enlisted as advisor and Hollick-Kenyon as pilot, Ellsworth set up base on Dundee Island off the tip of the Antarctic Peninsula.

Ellsworth and Hollick-Kenyon took off November 23 and headed south. Their cargo included emergency rations for two months. They needed almost all of it before their venture ended.

Halfway down the peninsula, Ellsworth sighted and named the Eternity Mountains. Other unmapped peaks appeared as they continued south, but later the plane reached a vast, unbroken plain of ice. For 1,000 miles, Ellsworth communicated with his base at Dundee Island. Then the plane's radio failed. They were still 1,300 miles short of their destination at Little America. Soon after this, more new mountains appeared. Then fog suddenly cut visibility. Ellsworth told Hollick-Kenyon to land. The pilot set the plane down on an undulating field of ice 6,400 feet above sea level.

In thirteen hours they had reached the heart of Marie Byrd Land.

Ellsworth later wrote that the monotony of the landscape got on his nerves, making him happy to crawl into the confines of the tent. The weather held them down for nineteen hours. During the wait, Ellsworth raised the Stars and Stripes on a staff and claimed the region for the United States.

The next hop of their flight lasted just half an hour. Thick weather grounded them in their second camp for three days. When they finally took off once more, it was again just a short hop. This time they camped on the ice for eight days, waiting for a blizzard to blow itself out. Ellsworth spent an entire day inside the plane on his stomach, scooping out windblown snow with a teacup.

The men grew impatient and finally took off even though visibility remained poor. They flew into clearing weather until Ellsworth wanted to stop for position check. They were 150 miles from the Bay of Whales. Next morning they took off, but before they could reach Byrd's base, the gas tanks ran dry, and they had to walk the rest of the way. Ellsworth and Hollick-Kenyon broke a skylight to enter one of the abandoned buildings at Little America. There they camped in relative comfort until Ellsworth's ship arrived to pick them up.

The flight, one of the boldest yet in Antarctic exploration, added new information about Marie Byrd Land and helped the United States come to grips with the issue of claims in the southern continent.

For many years, our government had stayed out of the land-grabbing game played by many other countries. The continental map had been cut up like a pie. New Zealand claimed the Victoria Land coast and Ross Ice Shelf. Australia claimed a large slice from Victoria Land to Enderby Land, territory broken only by a small wedge claimed by France at the Adelie coast. Norway claimed Queen Maud Land up to the eastern ridge of the Weddell Sea, and in a competition that would eventually come close to war, Chile, Argentina, and Britain all claimed the Antarctic Peninsula. The only unclaimed region of the continent was Marie Byrd Land.

For many years, the policy of 1924, as stated by Secretary of State Charles Evans Hughes, served as a convenient guide for the United States. This said claims alone did not establish sovereignty unless followed by actual settlement. Thus, while we claimed no ownership ourselves, we were not bound to recognize claims of other nations. By 1939, however, with Germany threatening global war, Antarctic claims took on new significance. The United States decided it must protect the work already done by Byrd and Ellsworth. For the first time since the Wilkes expedition of a hundred years before, Congress appropriated money for an Antarctic expedition. It was to be called the United States Antarctic Service. Byrd would be its leader.

The main thrust of the expedition would be geographic exploration, but sledge parties were to leave canisters containing claims at strategic spots and planes were to drop similar canisters during flights. These acts were to be recorded, but given no publicity. Our government wanted to establish a firm foundation without attracting contenders.

The choice of Byrd as leader was obvious. He had managed two productive expeditions without losing a man.

Scientists and others who had previously served under him made up our nation's only group of Antarctic experts, and more important, these men were anxious to serve under Byrd again.

The United States Antarctic Service moved south in 1940.

Despite Congressional support—$350,000 from the War and Navy departments and $327,000 in government equipment—Byrd still had to raise $240,000 from private sources to complete the financing of the expedition. Among private donations was a twenty-by-fifty-foot vehicle housing a laboratory, machine shop, photo dark room, chart room, living quarters, and kitchen. This thirty-three-and-a-half-ton Snow Cruiser, as it was called, was carried south as deck cargo and unloaded on the ice at the Bay of Whales. Its electric motors moved the monster well along level, hard ice, but on the slightest climb, where the surface turned soft with snow, the machine bogged down. The Snow Cruiser proved to be the biggest disappointment of the expedition. Instead of providing transport to the South Pole, as its inventors had hoped, the machine stood near Little America III, a monument to miscalculation.

Expedition plans called for two bases, one on the west, the other on the east of the Marie Byrd Land coast. The Bay of Whales, even though it lay in the sector claimed by New Zealand, provided the best harbor for the west base. Prefabricated buildings went up five miles north of the site of Little Americas I and II. Location of the eastern base proved more difficult.

Using *Bear*, a veteran polar ship that Byrd had sold to the Navy for one dollar as a personal contribution to the expedition, the staff for eastern base managed to get no more than

140 miles beyond Cape Colbeck at the tip of the King Edward VII Peninsula before ice stopped them. Seaplane surveys showed that Sulzberger Bay was much larger than originally suspected, but the plane could not pick out enough open leads for the *Bear* to progress further.

While *Bear*'s crew searched for a passage east, men at Little America III, who were not busy unloading stores and erecting buildings, worked hard to prepare aircraft for flight. A Curtiss-Wright Condor made two long flights before the southern summer ended. One flight brought back aerial photos of the region of Marie Byrd Land to be visited by trail crews the next spring. A second flight scouted the Transantarctic Mountains from Beardmore Glacier eastward and came upon another huge river of ice that is known today as Shackleton Glacier. This flight ended the season. On April 21, the sun set, not to rise again for 123 days.

Meanwhile, the *Bear,* after sailing far to sea to skirt the ice, landed thirty-three men and supplies for East Base on Stonington Island halfway down the west coast of the Antarctic Peninsula. Byrd had hoped to get closer to the unclaimed territory, but ice had blocked him. Search for a base, however, had been productive. Seaplane flights led to the discovery of Thurston Island, and several miles of adjacent coast were charted for the first time.

East Base, under command of Richard B. Black, had two major assignments. One sledge team would cross the peninsula and survey the ice-bound east coast. A second party would sledge south and explore the uncharted coast of eastern Marie Byrd Land.

As winter closed in, men of both bases paid special attention to their radios. War was sweeping Europe. Nazi armies had taken Norway, the Netherlands, and France. It seemed certain that the United States would soon be involved, but for men with a bare foothold on nature's most hostile continent, war seemed senseless and unreal. The men of the United States Antarctic Service lived in a remote world of their own, with their own hopes and their own troubles.

A midwinter fire nearly wiped out Little America III. The fire started in "Blubber House," a shed where men butchered seals for dog food. The blubber flamed like a torch in the cold wind. Fire is particularly feared in the Antarctic because it is impossible to keep a large supply of unfrozen water at hand to fight flames. The inferno filled tunnels and dog kennels with smoke. Stumbling in the dark, men probed through the snow searching for the buried kennels. Fortunately, they were found in time, and two men risked their lives by dropping into the smoke-filled passageways and handing up dogs. Many animals seemed near death, but fresh air revived them all, and the coming program of sledging was saved. Before the fire spread to other buildings, men with snow shovels managed to snuff it out.

One winter project at Little America called for altitude measurements of aurora. In the north, displays had been measured from fifty to three hundred miles above the earth, but measurements, though planned during Byrd's second expedition, had never been completed in the Antarctic. Three men, struggling through terrible winds and cold, set up an observatory fifteen miles from Little America. They had a camera mounted on a theodolite, a device that measured angles of direction and elevation. Through their radio set, they could make their observations coincide with those made at Little America.

At their tent camp, the temperature dropped to −71° F. Each time they exhaled, the moisture in their breath froze with a pop. It sounded like a soda bottle being opened. After eight days of misery, the three hurried back to base with their exposed film, or rather with film they thought was exposed. In the base dark room, workers found blanks. The shutter of the camera had been frozen shut through it all. The three, with remarkable dedication to their science, returned to their lonely outpost and repeated the entire series of observations. This time they were successful.

Unusually cold weather delayed the start of sledging parties until October 15. Then several teams fanned out from Little America into Marie Byrd Land. In less than three months these teams covered more territory than any previous Antarctic expedition. One team, specializing in geology, marched 796 miles, visited fifty-nine peaks, and raised the Stars and Stripes on all but two of them.

A biological team covered 725 miles, deposited claims as far away as the northernmost peak in the Edsel Ford Ranges and discovered the densest plant growth yet known on the continent. Lichens were so thick on some rocks, it appeared as if the rocks had grown curly heads of hair. The men could not explain why other rocks nearby, exposed to the same climate, had no growth at all.

The survey party covered the greatest distance of all— 1,200 miles—and it, too, left claims all along its route. The men found that Mount Hal Flood, sighted seven years earlier, was actually a series of peaks running to the east for eighty miles. Some of the peaks were more than 10,000 feet high. Beyond this discovery, the Condor later in the season reached an extinct volcano. Mount Siple, as it is now called, stands 10,200 feet above the shore. Several miles inland, the fliers sighted yet another range with an even higher peak. What they saw was the Executive Committee Range topped by Mount Sidley, 13,850 feet above sea level.

The achievement of the trail parties would not have been possible without effective motor transport, air support, and radio. Man had learned to combine all available technology for the assault on the southern continent.

With a milder climate, the men at East Base were able to do more work during the winter than those at Little America. Depots were set up in preparation for the summer campaign and a winter weather station was manned on the crest of the Peninsula east of Stonington Island. Men at the weather station launched twenty-five balloons and gathered valuable information on currents in the upper air.

In November, a three-man trail party led by Paul Knowles left Stonington Island, crossed the peninsula, and worked south along the shore of the Weddell Sea. Knowles and his men reached 71° 51' south latitude, and even though it was territory claimed by three other nations, Knowles left several claim sheets in rock cairns along his route. After a fifty-nine-day march, covering 683 miles, the men returned to East Base with numerous photos, twenty-two rocks, and the survey of a coastline that had never before been charted.

To start the southern march, seven men, fifty-five dogs, and 4,850 pounds of supplies were airlifted to the Wordie Ice Shelf one hundred miles south of Stonington Island. Two of the seven turned back after helping to establish supply depots. Three men, headed by J. Glenn Dyer, climbed inland to explore Ellsworth's Eternity Mountains while Finn Ronne and Carl Eklund continued south along the west coast of the

Antarctic Peninsula. Ronne, in charge of the two-man party, had been on Byrd's second Antarctic expedition.

The two men marched 1,200 miles in eighty-four days, explored the continental coast facing Alexander Island and proved that the land mass definitely was an island, separated from the mainland by iced-over George VI Sound. They were sixty miles from the border of unclaimed territory when food shortage and tired sledge dogs forced them to turn back. Ronne and Eklund brought home rock samples and data on twelve survey reference points which allowed them to fix the position of 320 peaks they had sighted during the journey.

In one summer of exploration, the United States Antarctic Service had accomplished great things, but when the summer ended, Byrd and his aides knew time had run out. America was at war.

Americans would not return to Antarctica until peace returned to the world, but other nations came to the peninsula and the claims dispute very nearly started war in Antarctica.

Early in 1943, a British ship visiting Deception Island found a plaque there claiming all the peninsula and the Weddell Sea for Argentina. Argentina favored Germany, and the British sailors considered the plaque a serious threat in the world conflict. They took it down and left a notice stating that Deception Island was the property of the British Crown. A year later, when the British returned to set up a base at Deception Island, their notice was gone and an Argentine flag had been painted on a rock. That emblem was soon covered by the Union Jack. Had the dispute remained at this level, it would have been harmless, but by the time peace came to the rest of the world, Antarctic battle lines had formed.

England said the peninsula and Weddell Sea were hers as part of the Falkland Islands Dependencies. Chile and Argentina charged England with imperialism and said England's claim conflicted with a papal bull of 1493 granting lands of the New World to Spain. The season of 1947–48 brought a crisis. The Argentine navy entered the harbor at Deception Island and anchored. While five men of the British base looked on, the Argentines established an outpost of their own. Responding to frantic radio messages, England sent a cruiser and a frigate south. Fortunately, neither side wanted war.

Chile, meanwhile, made a unique move to underline its claim. Gabriel Gonzalez Videla became the first head of state to visit Antarctica. He landed on Cape Legoupil while a band played and detachments of the Chilean army and navy stood at attention. There was even a twenty-one-gun salute. The impressive ceremony marked the opening of a new Chilean outpost.

All three countries were rapidly establishing new stations, more for sovereign interest than for advancement of science. Early in 1952, a British expedition arrived at Hope Bay at the tip of the peninsula to rebuild a station that had burned four years before. Argentina had built a station there during the British absence. The Argentines told the Englishmen not to land. The English ignored the warning. A burst of machine-gun fire whistled overhead. Hastily the Englishmen returned to their ship and radioed for help. England made diplomatic protest to Argentina, and Argentina answered that the incident was an unfortunate mistake and would not be repeated. The unloading operation resumed without further trouble and another base was established.

By 1955, England had seven bases and fifty men; Argentina had six bases and sixty-eight men; and Chile had four bases and twenty-nine men on the Antarctic Peninsula. England tried to take the dispute to the International Court of Justice in The Hague, but Chile and Argentina declared they would ignore any decision of the court. While the number of bases has since declined, the dispute remains unsettled to this day.

United States interest in Antarctica revived soon after the Japanese surrender. Military pressure contributed greatly to the revival. Both the army and the navy had developed new equipment during the war. Generals and admirals were anxious to have new ships and land vehicles tested in the polar regions. In 1946, the navy conducted Operation Nanook in Arctic waters, but fears grew in Washington that America might be accused of threatening other nations bordering on the Arctic. Operations in the Antarctic would bring less chance of criticism.

A bureaucratic reality also played a part in reviving interest in exploration. With the war over, our military leaders knew that an economy-minded Congress would soon be at work cutting military budgets. The best way to limit reductions was to put men and equipment to work on some new project.

All this post-war reasoning suited Admiral Byrd perfectly. He outlined plans for a new undertaking that became known as Operation Highjump. The army, the air force, and the navy all endorsed it. Highjump grew into the largest Antarctic expedition yet, involving 4,700 men and thirteen ships, including a submarine and an aircraft carrier. With nineteen planes and four helicopters, Byrd hoped to map the entire 16,000-mile coastline of Antarctica.

The force was divided into three groups. The Eastern and Western groups would operate with seaplane tenders and Martin Mariner seaplanes. The tenders would cruise off the coast. They would lower their planes by derrick, and the planes would make as many surveys as the weather allowed. The Central group would establish an airport on the ice at Little America, and send out Douglas DC3 planes for aerial survey.

Byrd took over-all command of Highjump. Operational command went to Rear Admiral Richard H. Cruzen who had served as captain of *Bear* during the Antarctic Service. George J. Dufek, who had been navigation officer of *Bear,* was put in charge of Eastern group. Siple, named scientific and polar adviser, also served as senior officer for the war department.

Central group, starting south on December 2, 1946, ran into difficulties as soon as it met the pack. While ships of the Western and Eastern groups could operate outside the pack, the Central fleet had to get through quickly in order to set up base at Little America. The year, however, was one of unusually heavy ice. The Coast Guard icebreaker *Northwind* scurried back and forth like a sheep dog herding a reluctant flock. While she freed one ship from ice, another ship called for help. By the time the fleet got through, operations of Central group had been seriously delayed.

Operation from the seaplane tenders, however, got underway December 29, when Dufek, on the tender *Pine Island,* sent up his first flight. The Martin Mariner was aloft ten hours and returned with photos of the coast near Thurston Island. The plane took off again as soon as it could be refueled and manned with a fresh crew of nine. Dufek knew he must work fast while good weather lasted, but he soon regretted launching the second flight. Clouds moved down on the coast at about the same time the Mariner arrived there. The barometer dropped. The radioman on the seaplane tender took down a report on the deteriorating weather from the plane. Then the plane's signal went dead. It had fuel enough to stay aloft twelve hours, but long before that period ended, Dufek knew his plane was in trouble. The storm struck *Pine Island,* making search flights impossible. Twelve days passed before Dufek could send up another plane; even then, the Mariner had to taxi to the lee of an iceberg to find enough smooth water to get aloft.

In four hours, men in the search plane sighted the wreckage of the missing Mariner on Thurston Island. There were survivors, but a message in the snow told that three men had died in the crash. Messages were dropped to the survivors, giving the direction to the nearest open sea. The men on the ground, many of them injured, began a difficult ten-mile walk.

Pilot Ralph Paul LeBlanc, with a badly burned face and hands, was the most seriously injured. Another man had a broken arm, but they all managed to reach the water where a seaplane waited. Buried behind in the snow, they left the bodies of navigator Maxwell Lopez, radioman Wendell Hendersin, and machinist mate Frederick Williams, the first men lost since Byrd began his Antarctic campaigns.

The survivors, once safely on the ship, told how they started to turn away from the storm when the horizon vanished in a white-out. The plane lost altitude on its turn and slammed into the ice. The fuselage broke in half, scattering men, emergency food, tents, and sleeping bags for hundreds of feet. The uninjured gathered up what they could find and made camp in the tail section of the plane.

Work went ahead. Eastern group made a total of twenty-one flights, collected nine thousand photos, and discovered a large inlet just west of Thurston Island. It is called Pine Island Bay.

The Western group, with *Currituck,* sister ship of the *Pine Island,* began aerial mapping at Victoria Land. As the ship worked westward, strong winds caused problems. Skies were clear, but spray, snow, and ice whipped up by the winds blurred the landscape, making clear photos impossible. Fortunately this condition did not last.

At first, the coast was backed by many high peaks, but later the peaks gave way to ice, rising in blocks and cracks to the inland plateau. At Vincennes Bay, pilots sighted nearly one hundred square miles of ice-free ground, and farther west, just beyond the Shackleton Ice Shelf, three hundred square miles of bare ground appeared. This region has been given the name Bunger Hills, honoring Highjump pilot David Eli Bunger who first sighted it.

The find, referred to as an oasis by newsmen, received more publicity than any other Highjump discovery. In a second flight, Bunger landed on one of the many lakes in the area, found it was salt water, and noted a stark absence of any life. Most lakes of Bunger Hills were later found to be fjords blocked off from the sea by arms of ice.

On February 22, 1947, with *Currituck* off Queen Maud Land, airmen discovered a new mountain range some one hundred miles from the coast. Peaks rose to eleven thousand feet. Glaciers oozed through passes and valleys from the high plateau beyond. This range has since been named the Sör Rondane Mountains. The Western group made thirty-four flights and produced forty thousand aerial photos. Its surveys extended from Victoria Land to the shores of the Weddell Sea, an arc embracing half the continent.

Among the first landed at Little America by the Central group were 168 Navy Seabees. They set to work at once leveling and packing an airstrip 5,000 feet long and 150 feet wide. These construction men, many with war experience on Pacific islands, knew how to do a job in a hurry. By January 30, 1947, all was ready, and 700 miles off shore an experiment began.

The aircraft carrier *Philippine Sea* carried six Douglas DC3s that would operate from Little America. They were equipped with jet boosters for take-off and a unique new landing gear, skis with slots holding wheels. Byrd rode in the first plane off the carrier's deck. The others followed without difficulty, and all pilots set their course by the radio beacon from Little America. The new gear worked perfectly as the planes landed one after the other on the hastily built runway. The day after the planes arrived, a blizzard struck.

It was already late in the season for flying. The men of Little America huddled in tents, waiting for the weather to improve. Since no one would be spending the winter this time, there were no snug houses connected by sheltered passages as before. Instead, the men of Highjump occupied a tent city.

On February 13, the flights began. As it turned out, the Antarctic allowed just fifty hours of clear weather, but in that time forty-six flights took place that produced twenty-one thousand photos. Pilots ranged west to Queen Victoria Land and east over Marie Byrd Land, almost connecting with the southern limit of Dufek's flights. One flight from Little America went to the South Pole and beyond by one hundred miles. When over the pole, Byrd dropped a canister containing all the flags of the United Nations. Another flight over Mount Markham in the Transantarctic Mountains revealed a huge, three-pronged glacier which the fliers thought bigger than any seen so far. Byrd Glacier it is called today.

During the flights, ground parties, with a variety of tracked vehicles developed during the war, traveled over the ice shelf and into Marie Byrd Land. Another war invention that proved useful in the Antarctic was the magnetometer. It had been developed to lead search planes to submerged U-boats, but its sensors could also pick up the magnetic field of submerged rock formations. Thus, if the rock below contained enough iron, a plane or ground vehicle could read the contours beneath the ice. Unfortunately, the instrument could not record sandstone and other nonferrous formations.

Another instrument recorded pulsations of terrestrial magnetism and kept a continuous record of these variations, a finer, more accurate record than any kept before.

Approaching winter forced all operations to close down, and on February 23, with gathering ice already posing a threat, Cruzen's ships took aboard all the men of Little America. The tent city and the planes that had served them so well were left to the elements.

Together, the three groups of Operation Highjump had surveyed an area more than half the size of the United States.

The seventy thousand photos would keep scholars and map-makers occupied for years.

There was one major fault with the survey—the same difficulty Wilkins had found in the first Antarctic flights. Without well-surveyed reference points, photos could be useless in mapping the continent. At the end of the operation, Highjump fliers were already having difficulty sorting and identifying their photos. The problem prompted a new American effort for the following season. Operation Windmill should really be considered an extension of Highjump. Two Navy icebreakers, *Burton Island* and *Edisto,* equipped with helicopters, landed survey teams around the Antarctic coast at key locations to establish benchmark positions. With this work accomplished, most of the Highjump photos could be fitted into their proper place in the growing map of the continent.

For Byrd, the Highjump and Windmill operations showed spectacular progress since his first Antarctic venture. He could look upon them with pride, for if any man deserved credit for that progress, it was he.

While the continent had attracted Byrd and others bent on discovery, the waters around Antarctica had attracted a different breed of men in the nineteenth century. These were the whalers and sealers.

13

Southern Whaling

JUST OUTSIDE THE drifting ice that rings Antarctica during the summer months, the water turns murky with plankton. Huge red patches mark the feeding krill. The krill attract fish, penguins, seals, and whales. This is the Antarctic Convergence. It teems with life.

We lack full understanding of the phenomenon, but we do know that the meeting of warm water with polar water lifts phosphates and nitrates to the sunlit surface of the sea. These compounds, in combination with the sun, spark the magic of life. Some students of the convergence believe it is the source of all ocean life. Others believe ocean currents of the world begin here. The currents of the region are puzzling.

Sea ice rarely drifts north of the convergence, but the bergs calved from ice shelf or glacier often travel far beyond, reaching the coast of Argentina, the southern tip of Africa, and the offshore waters of New Zealand and Tasmania. Somehow the deeper floating bergs are carried by currents that do not move the shallower sea ice across the line of convergence.

It is one of nature's contradictions that a continent so hostile to warmblooded animals should be surrounded by a sea of life where penguins, seals, and whales can thrive. The nearby ice affords an ideal platform. Here the seals and penguins can rest from their feeding. Many varieties never visit the land. They breed and raise their young on the ice. Whales once took shelter beneath the ice to escape from man, but that rarely occurs today. The whales are so rare that whaling is all but over. What happened?

The story of whaling in Antarctic waters followed the same pattern of senseless slaughter that virtually finished Arctic whaling. The difference was that when man started hunting in the Southern Ocean, as whalers called it, he had become a more efficient killer than ever before.

More whales were killed in forty-eight years of Antarctic whaling than were killed throughout the rest of the world in the previous four centuries. While a hundred men on an old New Bedford whaler might take and render one whale a month, just a few men aboard a modern catcher could harpoon twenty whales in one day, and seven hundred men on a modern factory ship could process fifty whales in twenty-four hours.

In less than one generation of man, the blue whale, biggest of all animals, bigger even than dinosaurs, was brought to the brink of extinction. At the start of the twentieth century, at least 100,000 blue whales populated the Southern Ocean. Today, there are no more than one thousand, and even though the blues have finally been protected, biologists fear the animals will die off faster than they can reproduce.

The first step in development of modern whaling came in 1885 when Svend Foyn, an inventive Norwegian whaler, took a new weapon to sea aboard the ship *Spes et Fides* (*Hope and Confidence*). At the bow stood a thick-barreled gun on a swivel. It shot a six-foot steel harpoon tipped with an explosive grenade. When the delayed action fuse ignited this bomb within the whale, the beast was either stunned into submission or killed instantly. The days of battle with a harpooned whale, the "Nantucket sleigh ride," and all other high excitement and risk ended with the development of the Svend Foyn gun.

Mounted on the bow of a fast steamship, the new gun enabled man to hunt any whale, even the speedy rorquals that had long been safe from the slow ships and rowboats of the early days. The rorqual family includes blue, fin, humpback, sei, and piked whales. Though some roamed far, the big populations were concentrated around Antarctica.

The blue whale, growing in rare cases to one hundred feet in length, has no match in size. When hunters were allowed to catch them, there was a rule that none under seventy feet could be harpooned—an impressive size limit for any fisherman.

The blues were found in two regions. One group fed in the Roaring Forties far from the Antarctic coast, while another group, perhaps a different breed, fed close to the ice pack, often surfacing in pools and leads beyond the reach of harpooners. The blues, while they lasted, were the biggest prize in whaling, yielding good oil and bringing about $6,000 each in gross profit.

The smaller fin whale, averaging between sixty and seventy feet, was counted half the equal of a blue whale, but it was profitably hunted well after the population of blue whales gave out. The fins generally feed farther from the ice than the southern blue whales.

The sei whale averages little over fifty feet. Whalemen figured it took six seis to equal one blue whale. The humpback, though shorter than the sei, yielded more oil. Two and a half humpbacks equaled one blue whale. The humpback was one of the first to be depleted. Once there were 34,000. Today there are 2,000 at the most.

The piked whale, about twenty-seven feet long, was the smallest taken by southern hunters. Generally, it was ignored when other whales were available. Today, with hunting virtually over, the piked whale populations appear to be increasing in the Southern Ocean.

In addition to rorqual whales, male sperm whales were sometimes taken in the Antarctic. Though the oil from the bachelor bulls was of good quality, the meat of the sperm whale was not worth packaging even for pet food. All was boiled in the cookers to extract oil.

For whalers, the chief difference between rorquals and other whales was their speed and low buoyancy. Rorquals can swim at twenty knots and sprint even faster. In addition, they sink soon after being killed. The steamship solved the speed problem, and the Svend Foyn gun, with a barbed harpoon triggering open inside the whale, solved the sinking problem. The strong grip of the harpoon could hold the whale on the surface until compressed air was forced into the carcass to make it float.

In the north, development of the Svend Foyn gun revived the whaling industry. Whalers had a new species to hunt. Coastal factories on Norway, Labrador, Iceland, and the Faroes were soon producing millions of barrels of whale oil. Men who invested in whale catchers and factories amassed fortunes in two or three years, but as might be expected, the success attracted more and more whalers. The fleet of catchers grew. The northern rorquals rapidly decreased. There was no restraint, no talk of controlling the harvest. By the end of the nineteenth century, the whaling revival had ended. The only untapped region of whaling left in the world was the Antarctic.

In 1892, Norwegian whaling skipper Carl A. Larsen sailed to the Southern Ocean and found an abundance of whales. He returned the next season, but his ship, *Jason,* was not fast enough to catch rorquals. Larsen came south again in 1901 as captain of the Swedish expedition's *Antarctica.* Though he lost his ship in the ice, Larsen returned to Norway with big plans. He talked at length of the bounty of Antarctic waters, but he could find no one in Norway willing to finance a whaling venture so far from home. In the end, Larsen enlisted businessmen in Argentina for his venture. Compania Argentina de Pesca thus became the first firm to build a whaling factory on South Georgia Island.

South Georgia lies on the edge of the Antarctic Convergence. Catchers did not have to search far for whales. The hunt began in December of 1904 and was an immediate success. Investors in Norway who had turned Larsen away a few months before suddenly became interested in the new whaling grounds. English and Scottish investors also entered the picture. By 1911, eight whaling stations operated on South Georgia Island under lease agreement with Britain's Falkland Islands Dependencies. A ninth station operated on Deception Island to the southwest.

The harbor of Deception Island, an inundated crater of an extinct valcano, was an exceptional shelter, but other islands off the Antarctic coast offered hazardous anchorage, unsuitable for coastal whaling factories. Catchers, however, ranged farther and farther from the stations. The industry needed a new approach—floating factories.

The first factory ships were old freighters converted to handle whales. As in the old days, the carcasses were cut up along one side of the ship, and the blubber was hoisted aboard to be rendered in try pots on deck. These vessels provided mobility, but they were still unable to operate in rough water. They needed shelter.

While the industry was in this stage, England could control whaling in the Southern Ocean. The whaling stations and the islands offering the necessary shelter were all under her control. England limited the number of whale catchers operating each year and banned taking female whales with calves. In addition, England levied a tax on whale oil. Revenue from this taxation financed research on whales. This program made good sense. Further controls would be based squarely on research. Unfortunately, it took years for researchers to get their questions answered.

During World War I, the demand for explosives soared. Explosive could be made from glycerine, and glycerine came from animal fat. England lifted the controls on southern whaling, and catch in the 1915–16 season rose to 11,792 whales. Controls were reinstated after the war, however, and in 1926, England sent *Discovery,* Scott's famous ship, on a scientific cruise to the whaling grounds. It was the start of a series of cruises which would be followed by the English research vessels *William Scoresby* and *Discovery II,* but the research started too late.

When the *Discovery* first sailed, change had already started among the whaling fleets. Companies had begun launching strange vessels. They looked like two big tankers side by side. A wide gateway and ramp split the stern. The ramp led to a tunnel beneath the housing of the afterdeck, and beyond to an open arena. The midship housing stood on an archway leading to the foredeck and another arena. It was a huge butcher shop.

Below decks were automatic cutters, pressure cookers, centrifuge tanks, and ovens. These whale factories could operate on the open sea, beyond the shelter of the islands controlled by England. The modern factory ship allowed whalers to escape control.

A fleet of twelve or more speedy catchers, each armed with a Svend Foyn gun, served one factory. During the 1930–31 whaling season, just four years after the work of *Discovery* began, more than 40,000 whales were taken in the Southern Ocean and only 2,736 of these were processed through the South Georgia Island factories.

A factory ship with its fleet of catchers entered the whaling grounds as a highly organized unit. The factory ship skipper directed his catchers by radio. When one catcher located good hunting, other ships were sent speeding toward the area.

As long as there were whales, the hunt pressed on. It began in the old way with a call from the lookout at the masthead of the catcher. The alarm alerted men on the bridge and the harpooner and his assistant hurried down the ramp to the bow. Quickly, the two men took the canvas cover from the gun. The harpooner released the swivel lock and made sure the gun turned freely. He also made certain that the harpoon line leading to the locker below deck was clear.

The all-important harpooners, highest paid men in the whaling fleet, usually served as skippers of the catchers. As the hunt closed, they directed the helmsman, controlling both speed and direction of the catcher through hand signals.

The whales, though frightened, most often stuck together in small herds as they tried to flee from the speedy ship. The harpooner would try for the biggest whale in the herd. Often it was a difficult task to bring the ship within range. The whales might slow without warning. If the harpooner and the man at the helm were not alert, the catcher might pass the herd before a shot could be fired. The herd could also turn quickly, and if it should scatter, the harpooner had to decide at once what turn to take, which beast to single out for slaughter.

Aiming the harpoon took skill and experience, particularly in rough water, but most veteran harpooners rarely missed. The boom of the gun would shake the small ship. The harpoon traveled almost too swiftly for the eye to follow, but the trailing harpoon line marked its course. Sixty feet was considered a long shot. Usually, the harpooner tried to get closer before pulling the trigger.

Right after the harpoon struck home, a thud would sound

within the whale. This was the grenade exploding. The boat's strong winch would then crank up the line, drawing the whale closer. The harpooner and his assistant, meanwhile, would reload their gun. Sometimes a second shot was needed to finish the beast, but the hunters tried to avoid this. They got complaints enough from the factory ship about the iron fragments in flesh and blubber from one grenade. The fragments dulled cutting knives and jammed machinery.

When the whale was drawn beside the catcher, a man reached over the rail and pierced the body with a long tube. Compressed air was then pumped into the whale, making it float higher and higher in the water. During this process, other workers with sharp knives on long handles reached down to cut off the whale's flukes. Still other men attached a marker buoy to identify ownership of the whale, and in recent times, a small radio transmitter was attached to guide the pick-up boat.

On the masthead, the lookout remained watching other whales in the herd. As soon as the catcher could cast its whale loose, the chase resumed. The drifting whale might be picked up later in the day by the catcher that killed it, or it might be taken to the factory ship by a buoy boat assigned the job of following the catchers to collect the harvest. Flukes of the dead whale had to be removed to keep the whale from "swimming" from its position. Even in death the undulation of the huge flukes could drive the carcass many miles before a pick-up boat reached the scene.

The entire process, from sighting of the whale to casting off its buoyed and trimmed carcass, might have consumed no more than ten minutes. It was not difficult for the catcher to keep up with a herd, killing as it went.

Chase of a lone whale was more difficult. Its course was less predictable, but in the hunting era after World War II, catchers carried sonar gear to track the whale even when it sounded.

At the end of the hunt, the dead whales, collected either by catcher or buoy boat, were delivered to the factory ship which had followed in the wake of its fleet. After the transfer of lines, the dead whales floated in the stern of the big ship, waiting their turn to be hauled aboard. Lifting a whale of one hundred tons or more up the sloping ramp in the stern of the factory ship was made possible by another Norwegian invention, the *hval kla,* a giant hand of steel, swung out on cables to clamp the stump of the whale's tail. As winches groaned under the strain, the huge carcass rose, and gradually slid up the ramp onto the open deck. Even before it stopped moving, flensers went to work making long cuts down the whale's body from tail to head. The flensers carried sharp, curved knives with long handles, a tool looking much like a hockey stick. The cuts loosened long slabs or blankets of blubber which had to be lifted from the carcass by cable. While one crew of men cut these blankets into ten-foot strips, another crew with long hooks pulled and shoved the strips toward holes in the deck. These holes led to chopping machines that chunked the blubber, preparing it for the pressure cookers.

The whale carcass, once stripped of its blubber, traveled forward by winch to an area near the midship arch where another crew with knives, hooks, and cables jerked the baleen from the whale's mouth. The rorqual baleen, shorter than the bone of right and bowhead whales, was one of the few things discarded by modern whalers. In an age of plastic, baleen had no value.

Beyond the arch, men called lemmers went to work with knives and steam-driven saws to complete the butchering process. Meat was removed expertly. Bones were sawed into sections small enough for the cookers. All parts went into special holes in the deck of the ship.

Below, where workers received various parts of the whale, the scene was just as active as above. Key to the efficiency of the floating butcher shop was the cooker, working on the same principle as the kitchen pressure cooker but far bigger. Developed for modern whaling by Nils Kvaerner, a Finnish engineer living in Oslo, these ten-by-twenty-foot cookers built up six hundred pounds pressure. Kvaerner cookers extracted the oil from flesh, blubber, and bone far faster and much more efficiently than the old try works. The oil floating to the top was drained off and the watery soup below was run through centrifuge tanks to catch the last droplets of oil. What remained was pumped to ovens to be dried and bagged for fertilizer.

Oil was still the prize; but it no longer served as fuel for lamps. It was used to make soap, glycerine, and margarine. Whale factories carried their own tanks for storing oil, but usually the tanker sent to refuel the fleet during the season filled its empty tanks with whale oil piped from the factory. Often meat was also transferred at sea to a storage or refrigerator ship operating with the fleet.

On most factory ships, some meat was cooked for its oil, with the better cuts going to the canning or freezing plants to be put up for pet food. On Russian and Japanese factories, however, the meat was prepared for human consumption. Whale meat is still a very important source of protein in Japan, one reason why the Japanese have continued whaling on the high seas.

In addition to meat and oil, factory ships also produced vitamin A extract from the whale's liver. Other glands and extracts provided raw material for perfume makers. The only part not used, besides the flukes and baleen, were the intestines of the whale. On the open sea, disposal of the intestines was no problem, but the coastal stations at South Georgia Island earned infamy for the smell rising from their disposal heaps. The odor of the island reached the downwind sailor long before the sparkling, snow-covered peaks of South Georgia came into view. Whalers referred to South Georgia as "the South Atlantic slum."

As slaughter of whales increased, some men, including a few farsighted whalers, knew restraints had to be imposed to save both the whales and the industry. First efforts at control were made under the League of Nations. The League appointed a whaling committee to formulate regulations, but World War II ended both the League of Nations and the committee. In 1946, however, members of the old committee and others formed the International Whaling Commission. It had representatives from fifteen nations and the help of many concerned scientists. The commission began to set annual quotas. It was never an easy job. The whaling companies always argued that quotas were too low. Too often, the whalers won the argument. In 1963, for instance, scientists said no more than four thousand fin whales should be killed if breeding stocks were to be maintained. That year, whalers took fourteen thousand fins.

The whale scientists once said sensible quotas and enforcement might produce stable populations that would permit a harvest of twenty-five thousand whales each year, but no nation could agree on such quotas or on an inspection system. Thus the commission, despite good intentions, could not save the whale.

The salvation, however, might yet come. Modern whaling is expensive, so expensive that companies cannot afford to send an expedition to waters where whales are scarce. Today, the few surviving whales in the Southern Ocean are generally unmolested. Russia and Japan, the two nations remaining in the factory-ship business, have found better whaling for the moment in other regions. If the whale populations do revive, it is possible, barely possible, that the men returning to southern waters will be wiser. To gain such wisdom, the experience of the recent years must be understood and remembered.

In 1954, there were ten Norwegian factory ships, two each from Scotland and Japan, and one each from England, South Africa, the Netherlands, and Russia hunting whales in the Southern Ocean. All eighteen of these ships produced profits for their owners. In 1958, Norwegian whalers alone took 31,000 whales. Ten years later, Anders Jahre[14] of Sandefjord, Norway, owner of the world's biggest fleet of whalers, reported that the annual catch had dropped to 15,000 small whales. In the same ten years, Norwegian whale-oil production had fallen from 106,000 to 10,800 tons. With such a small yield, Jahre said he could no longer stay in business. He was closing down. Today huge factory ships and the swift catchers lie idle in the anchorage at Sandefjord. The thousands of men who once made their living from the whale have had to find other occupations.

Though Antarctic whaling has ended, at least for our lifetime, men are still trying to learn more about whales. Scientists on the *Discovery* and other research vessels that followed have found that most whales leave the rich feeding grounds of the Antarctic Convergence in winter and migrate northward into warmer regions of the South Atlantic, South Pacific, and Indian oceans. For six months, the whales evidently do not feed at all.

We still lack full understanding of the breeding habits of whales, particularly the rorquals. Some sperm whale cows breed every two years, but most are on a four-year cycle. The term of pregnancy in sperm cows is sixteen months, and for two years after the calf is born, it nurses on its mother. It takes nine years for a sperm whale to reach sexual maturity and reproduce, but the sperm whale continues to grow for forty-five years.

How long does a whale live? No one can be sure. Seventy-five years is considered extremely old for a sperm whale, but the method of determining age is still uncertain. Scientists have counted the layers of hard wax laid down inside the whale's ear, thinking a new layer occurred once a year, but recent research has found that some whales produce two layers a year.

Though the sperm whale has been studied more than most, no one can yet explain the purpose of the oil reservoir in its head. Early whalers thought this spermaceti had something to do with reproduction—thus the name sperm whale—but this notion has been disproved. Today, scientists are working on the theory that the oil allows the sperm whale to dive to great depths without suffering from bends. Human divers can be crippled or killed by bubbles of nitrogen freed in the blood as pressure is released coming up from a dive. The spermaceti might absorb nitrogen, but no one has proved it yet.

What of the whale's intelligence? The dolphin, smallest of the whales, is the smartest creature of the sea, perhaps on a par with a chimpanzee, but the brain of this and other whales is remarkably small in relation to overall body size. Even the biggest whales, however, have shown a capacity to learn.

When whalers first entered the Southern Ocean early in this century, they found all whales easy to approach, almost tame. Within a few seasons, however, whales fled the boats. This shows learning as well as some form of communication. Whales that had never suffered the pain of a harpoon, perhaps had never seen a ship before, still fled. Observers repeatedly noted that large herds of whales usually sounded together, another suggestion of communication.

Whales make a variety of noises, ranging from bird-like chirps to low, prolonged groans, suggesting a heavy door swinging slowly on rusty hinges. In 1971 Roger S. Payne of Rockefeller University and Scott McVay of Princeton University published results of a study of humpback whale "songs" recorded by underwater microphones. Each whale had a distinct pattern of tones that sometimes lasted thirty minutes without interruption or repetition. The song of the humpback whale may serve as a means of identification. It may be a method of communication, or it may simply be sounds sent out to aid in underwater navigation. Echoes, bouncing back, could warn of obstruction. Payne and McVay conclude that the songs could serve any one or all of these functions.

Whale vision is not good, and the position of the eyes on each side of the head just behind the mouth does not give a view directly ahead. In the darkness of great depths, the sperm whale certainly uses some kind of echo system to avoid submarine crags and peaks as he hunts the giant squid.

For a long time, scientists could not explain how a whale could attain speeds of twenty knots and more. Tank tests using models of whales produced so much turbulence and friction that such speeds seemed impossible, but the tests were made with rigid models. When a model fashioned of rubber was run through a test tank, it was discovered that the turbulence and friction dropped sharply. The conclusion was that the whale's pliant skin and underlying blubber cushion the eddies of turbulence and allow the great speed.

Though the story of modern whaling has been one of destruction for the whales and the industry they supported, whaling contributed substantially to exploration of the Southern Continent. A whaleship helped Byrd get through the pack on his first expedition. Whalers have often stood by to aid or supply many other explorers. One Norwegian whaling family spent nearly as much energy on exploration as it did in pursuing the whales. Christen Christensen of Sandefjord financed Larsen's first whaling voyage south in 1892 and sent the first factory ship to the Southern Ocean in 1905. In 1923, a Christensen ship, under command of Larsen, forced a pack and became the first to take whales in the Ross Sea. Christensen's son, Lars, furthered the family's tradition of adventure. Lars, who sailed south with his wife on several expeditions, sent *Odd I,* a research vessel, to Antarctic waters to study whale migrations in 1926. The following year, he sent *Norvegia,* designed both for whaling and exploration. *Norvegia* sailed four seasons and during the last two carried a seaplane and veteran polar pilot Hjalmar Riiser-Larsen.

On December 7, 1929, less than a week after Byrd's polar flight, Riiser-Larsen made his first flight over the Antarctic coast. He landed near Enderby Land's Cape Ann, taxied to shore, and raised the flag of Norway. Mawson, however, was already in the area, making claims for Australia, so the *Norvegia* worked westward to avoid conflict. Riiser-Larsen charted much of the coast of Queen Maud Land, giving Norway foundation for the claim eventually made to the region, a region six times bigger than Norway.

In 1935, the Christensen tanker *Thorshavn,* supplying the whaling fleet with fuel, discovered an ice-free coast halfway between the Shackleton Ice Shelf and Enderby Land. Captain Klarius Mikkelsen, his wife, and seven crewmen rowed ashore in a small boat to investigate a shoreline of bays and inlets. Mrs. Mikkelsen became the first woman to set foot on the continent. Two years later, Lars Christensen and his wife, Ingrid, visited the same region. The Lars Christensen Coast and the Ingrid Christensen Coast, bordering the Amery Ice Shelf, were named in their honor.

Whaling prompted an ambitious German expedition in 1938. Hitler's Third Reich government wanted to establish rights to whaling grounds by making claim to a portion of the continent. The expedition, led by Alfred Ritscher, was to extend through two seasons. In the first season, seaplanes launched from off-shore ships made several long-range flights over Queen Maud Land, and cameramen mapped some 135,000 square miles of the continent. Hitler canceled the second ground survey phase of the expedition because of World War II.

14

Seals and Penguins

TODAY THERE ARE just three species of seals found on the Southern Continent. The Weddell, crabeater, and leopard seal have no commercial value and were thus spared the slaughter that began early in the last century.

The hunters first sought the Kerguelen fur seal, whose pelt was nearly equal in quality to the northern fur seal of the Pribilof Islands. With as many as thirty seal ships cruising the ice pack and offshore islands of Antarctica each season, it did not take long for fur-seal populations to decline. Hunters were senseless in their waste. Adult seals in an entire rookery were killed, leaving the pups to starve. The average catch per vessel in the beginning reached 57,000 pelts per season.

In 1822, the total kill was estimated at 1,250,000 seals. This did not include some 100,000 pups left to starve. By 1842, Antarctic fur-seal hunting was over. It had a brief revival in 1872, and in the sixteen years that followed hunters collected 45,000 pelts, but then the hunting stopped again, and the Kerguelen fur seal was thought extinct. In 1933, however, a small rookery was discovered on Bird Island off the northern tip of South Georgia, and under protection, the seals have since increased gradually. Today, there may be 33,000 in this colony.

When the fur seals first declined, hunters began slaughtering the southern elephant seal. Pelts of these huge, twenty-two-foot seals had no value, but the elephant seal was a fine source of oil. The hunting reached a peak in 1850; then these populations declined. By 1900 there were too few for profitable hunting. Since then, again with protection, the southern elephant seal has made an amazing recovery. There may be 700,000 on the islands surrounding the continent today with 300,000 on South Georgia Island alone.

Elephant seals got their name, not from their size, but because of a nose pouch that looks something like the trunk of an elephant, particularly when inflated. The purpose of the pouch is unclear, but it does add resonance to the seal's voice. The roar of an angry bull can be heard several miles. These non-migratory seals eat cuttlefish and other squid, diving up to ten minutes and to depths of two thousand feet to feed.

The elephant seal's only enemies, other than man, are the

killer whale, which takes both adults and pups, and the leopard seal, which kills pups. In rare cases, pups have also succumbed to the rapidly changing Antarctic weather. In a thaw, the ice under a dozing pup melts and his body sinks into a pocket. A sudden drop in temperature will freeze the melt water and hold the pup in a fatal trap.

Among the three non-commercial seals, the Weddell seal is most southerly. It is rarely found out of sight of the Antarctic mainland. The Weddell seal, tubby-shaped and some ten feet long, may weigh nine hundred pounds, with females slightly larger than males. There are about 500,000 of them.

They eat squid, shellfish, and fish and can dive for forty minutes to depths of two thousand feet. In winter the seals take to the water to escape the cold, but in southern summers, Weddell seals can usually be seen basking on the shore. In winter the seal uses its teeth to carve breathing holes in the ice. Teeth of older animals are badly worn. Injured, old, and sick Weddell seals have been known to travel far inland either to recover or die. This retiring instinct has been observed among other seals, but the Weddell's instinct is unusually strong. Some bodies have been found on inland glaciers three thousand feet above sea level.

The crabeater seal, smaller than the Weddell, weighs up to five hundred pounds. Crabeaters surround the southern continent, preferring ice to shore. There may be five million of them, making the crabeater the most populous southern seal. They feed exclusively on krill and their upper and lower teeth fit together closely to serve as a strain, rejecting water and retaining food.

Despite their numbers, little is known about the crabeaters. No more than a dozen have been observed closely. They breed in the pack during late winter or spring, a time when ships and men cannot reach them.

The leopard seal, numbering about 200,000, is an aggressive predator, feeding on pups of other seals and penguins. Its small head, long neck, and big mouth give this ten- to twelve-foot-long seal a snake-like appearance. It is slow on ice, but swift and deadly in the water. It has been known to leap ten feet in the air to snatch a penguin from the edge of an ice floe.

The Antarctic Convergence supports several varieties of penguins, including the marconi, Magellanic, and gentoo. Most of them live and breed on the ice or in the small islands surrounding Antarctica, but two varieties, the emperor and the Adelie penguin, spend part of each year on the continent.

Adelies arrive from the feeding grounds at the start of the southern summer and gather in huge rookeries along the coast. They stand about two feet high and have a glistening back of bluish-black and a white chest tinged with yellow. Their beaks are a dark orange; their eyes are yellow with black pupils.

The most impressive features of an Adelie rookery are noise and smell. The smell can be overpowering, the noise almost as bad. During the mating season, the birds rear their heads back, wave their flippers slowly, and begin a low, pulsating song that rises gradually in pitch until it reaches an ear-splitting climax. When a rookery of five thousand or more penguins raises its chorus, a wise man covers his ears.

The Adelies build nests of pebbles and the pebbles appear to be an important part of courtship. A male presents a pebble to the female, and she places it in the nest ring. Nests, however, are difficult to maintain because of thievery. The moment a penguin turns its back, other birds snatch pebbles from the nest. Once the eggs are laid, this frantic stealing stops. The female lays two eggs. Birds will sit on their nests for weeks at a time, through wind and snow, to keep the eggs from freezing.

During the IGY, naturalist Carl Eklund, Finn Ronne's companion on the long sledge journey across George VI Sound, implanted Adelie eggs with a telemetering device to record temperatures. The birds kept their eggs at between 84.5° and 98.2° F despite sub-zero weather.

After the hatch, however, chicks die by the thousands, either from freezing or by falling victim to the ever-present skua gulls. The parents feed the young by regurgitating food, but some chicks starve because their parents have built the nest too far inland. By the time a parent bird reaches the water, feeds, and returns to the nest it is too late to save the chicks. Chick losses among Adelies has been estimated at 68 percent.

The penguins often lose their way on land. Explorers have met some Adelies sixty to seventy miles inland, marching the wrong way from both rookery and coastline. In the sea, however, Adelies have a remarkable homing instinct. Five birds from a rookery near Wilkes Station, east of Shackleton Ice Shelf, were banded and taken to McMurdo Sound for release. Eleven months later, three of the banded birds were found back at the Wilkes Station rookery. They had swum 2,200 miles.

The emperor penguin, three feet tall and weighing ninety pounds, is the largest of all penguins and far more dignified in behavior than the clowning Adelie. While Adelies breed on the continent in the summer time, emperor penguins choose the dead of winter. Only three emperor rookeries are known, but there are certainly many more, perhaps one hundred. Man simply cannot travel far to search and study rookeries in the southern winter.

The best emperor study was made by a French expedition to Adelie Land in 1952. The first two penguins arrived at the rookery March 10, just at the start of winter. They were fat from feeding in the convergence. In two weeks, there were one hundred and ten well-fed birds on the shore ice. Then arrivals increased, reaching a rate of four hundred a day. Eventually, there were thirteen thousand penguins on the shore ice. The ice sagged under the load, and the French explorers noted that the flock broke up into small groups, evidently for better weight distribution.

The courtship of the penguins fascinated the observers. It was extremely formal. It began with the pair at attention, necks extended, and beaks pointed skyward. Next, the birds lowered their heads and rubbed their beaks with their flippers. Then, with heads pressed to their chests, the birds took deep breaths and began a long, complex love song, which ended with a high, sustained note. As the song ended, the birds assumed the original position of attention. Within a few moments, however, they began the ritual again. It took several days for the birds to pair. Sometimes females, whose songs differed markedly from the males, would wander about, apparently dissatisfied with all wooing. On other occasions, two females fought over a male. By April, the ritual grew more intense, with the birds standing rigidly at attention for long periods, refusing to budge even when the men touched them. The birds would give up their posing only when blizzards struck. Then they would gather in huddles, their backs to the wind. Chilled birds constantly worked toward the center of the huddle, forcing others out to serve as shields.

Egg laying began May 5 and continued two weeks. The female would roll the single, one-pound egg onto her feet and tuck it beneath the folds of fat in her lower abdomen. The egg, four inches in diameter, was hidden completely by the bird, but the day after laying it, the female would give it up to the male. The transfer involved another ritual. When the male arrived, identifying himself with his song, the female let the egg drop to her feet and roll onto the ice. The male then touched it with his beak, as if to make sure it was real. Then the male took charge, rolling the egg onto his own feet and tucking it into his pocket of fat. He kept it there until the egg hatched, a period of sixty-two days. The male might waddle about awkwardly, but he held the egg and never left the ice to feed. He stood exposed to the wind and snow in company with other brooding males.

When the males took charge, all females of the rookery left for the open sea. They would feed well while their mates fasted.

Throughout incubation, the Frenchmen noted many losses. Some males accidentally dropped their egg. If they were unable to retrieve it quickly, the egg froze. Popping of frozen eggs sounded daily. When the eggs finally hatched, there were further losses as the wind swept chicks from the parent's warm pocket. Many newly hatched birds died on the ice, while the adults searched for them. Frequently, a male without a chick tried to steal one from another male.

With uncanny timing, the females all returned soon after the eggs hatched, and the rookery became a bedlam as the birds sang their songs of identification. Often it took a female a full day to locate her mate, but once found, all attention went to the chick. It was fed food regurgitated by the female. With his mate returned, the male was free to feed once more. The French scientists figured that he had gone four months without food.

Zoologists do not agree on how the penguin evolved. Some believe it developed from a bird that could fly, the wings gradually modifying to serve as flippers. Others who have studied penguins say they are the most primitive of all birds and that a close study of penguin embryo development may give man a better understanding of how all birds evolved from reptiles. Whichever view is correct, penguins will continue to delight and fascinate men who visit Antarctica.

15

The Great Laboratory

SINCE MEN BEGAN sailing south, many discoveries, as we have seen, have been made in Antarctica. Many of them brought great changes in man's understanding of his world.

One of the more exciting discoveries is also one of the more recent. In 1969, a group of studious Americans armed with geological hammers and searching eyes established a new science on the Southern Continent—vertebrate paleontology, a study of the fossilized remains of highly developed animals.

Scott and his doomed comrades collected fossils from the

sandstone cliffs bordering Beardmore Glacier to prove that ferns once flourished on the continent, but for years, no one found anything to suggest the existence of any animal life other than primitive insects.

The first hint did not come until 1967 when New Zealand zoologist Peter J. Barrett, then a graduate student at Ohio State University, visited Antarctica with several other scientists for a season of research. In the Transantarctic Mountains, Barrett picked up a small piece of bone which appeared to be part of the skull of a fresh-water amphibian. The fragment, however, was too small for positive identification. Fellow scientists, in fact, still marvel that the fragment caught Barrett's attention.

Small as it was, the find prompted a special expedition to the continent.[15] Early in 1969, with backing from the National Science Foundation and Ohio State's Institute of Polar Studies, seventeen men set up camp near Coalsack Bluff, an outcrop of sandstone on the northeast side of the Queen Alexandra Range. Search of the area where Barrett made his find produced nothing, and with the approach of winter, the disappointed scientists were forced to retreat temporarily.

Next season the men returned, and expedition leader, Dr. David H. Elliot, picked a new search area just west of Coalsack Bluff. The men found fossils. Just four miles from camp, reptile and amphibian bones appeared in abundance. The delighted scientists spent the entire season collecting samples. They sought fragments large enough to identify with known species.

Paleontologists in a bone pile are happier than children in a toy shop. They sometimes forget their surroundings. This evidently was what happened to Brigham Young University's James A. Jensen on December 4, 1969. The weather turned colder than it had yet been during the expedition, but Jensen continued working on an exposed cliff. Again and again, he tapped fossils free from the sandstone and wrapped, bagged, and tagged each specimen. He continued working even after his hands turned stiff with cold. Hours after a less enthusiastic worker would have returned to the shelter of camp, Jensen's hammer split a rock to reveal a jawbone. It was an important find, but at that point Jensen was too numb for emotion. He simply gathered up his specimens and returned to camp. He handed his day's collection to Dr. Edwin H. Colbert, a veteran paleontologist, and went to the cook hut for a warm meal. Dr. Colbert, long associated with the American Museum of Natural History and now with the Museum of Northern Arizona at Flagstaff, examined the bones with an expert eye.

Moments later, he dashed into the hut. Jensen had found a *Lystrosaurus*. What is a *Lystrosaurus?* Why was Dr. Colbert excited about it?

It was a dog-sized reptile that lived in freshwater marshes 225 million years ago. One reason why Dr. Colbert and other scientists were excited over the find was that this was the first bone found in the Antarctic that could be identified with a specific species, but a second cause for excitement was the fact that the ancient jawbone confirmed a theory of geophysics which had been argued over by scholars for almost a century—the theory of continental drift.

Many remains of *Lystrosaurus* had already been found through Asia and Africa, but it was not a swimming reptile. Its presence four hundred miles from the South Pole proved that Antarctica, Asia, and Africa were once one continent, and over eons of time the continents had split and drifted apart, arriving close to their present locations before man evolved from the lower primates.

For Jensen work in Antarctica was over. The 52-year-old scientist had suffered dangerous frostbite and had to be flown home. His comrades worked through the rest of the season, but none matched his discovery. Jensen had not only quieted much debate among world scientists but had also opened new fields of inquiry.

Today, few men dispute the theory of continental drift. When Austrian geologist Eduard Suess suggested in 1885 that Africa, Madagascar, and the Indian Peninsula were once part of one continent he called Gondwanaland, he was generally ridiculed. Suess at one time added Australia and later South America to his concept of Gondwanaland. There were others who wrote of the idea. An American author is believed to have put forth the idea first in 1858, but the theory of continental drift did not become a serious subject for scientific debate until 1911 when Alfred Wegener, a highly respected German geophysics and meteorology professor, began writing books on the origin of the continents. Wegener, who was also a polar explorer, presented a thorough study of Gondwanaland, saying that it included South America, Africa, India, Australia, and Antarctica. Wegener's strongest criticism came from scientists who said he failed to explain the forces that caused the massive continents to move. However, criticism began to subside as field workers gathered more and more evidence showing that the lands involved often shared similar plant fossils and rock structures. In 1937, when South Africa's distinguished geologist Alexander L. du Toit[16] published *Our Wandering Continents,* the theory of continental drift gathered firm support from many leading thinkers.

Still, the notion that land masses drifted about on the surface of the earth like so many ice floes on a polar sea remained difficult for many men to accept, until, in 1968, the American research vessel *Glomar Challenger* returned from a cruise of the Atlantic with core samples of the ocean floor. The cores showed that South America and Africa have been drifting apart for from 180 to 230 million years and that this movement continues today. The core samples proved drift a reality, but they still did not confirm the notion of Gondwanaland. Confirmation came with the discovery of *Lystrosaurus's* jawbone in Antarctica. Today, even the most tradition-bound scholars believe that South America, Africa, India, Australia, and Antarctica were once joined.

The drift theory might not fully explain the coal and oil found in the polar regions. A much hotter climate than we have now might have been enough to bring on the lush growth that produced the carbon fuels, but there is also evidence that the poles themselves have migrated. Geologists tell us that an icecap once covered the Sahara Desert, and another spread over a vast region of the Pacific Ocean. These were most probably polar icecaps, but no one can say whether they existed in these areas because of continental drift, a shift in the poles, or a combination of both.

What forces cause the drift remain a mystery. One theory is that the molten magma that forms the earth's core is constantly surging and that this motion influences the earth's crust. Possibly the gravitational pull of the sun and moon, the cooling of the earth, or its daily rotation influence the drift.

Recent work suggests that earthquakes, the sudden release of tensions built up in the earth's crust, probably from continental movement, might be predicted through observations at the poles. The poles of spin, moving within a few feet of the geographic poles, wander. Some years they might be very close to the geographic poles, but other years the distance increases by several feet. In other words, the earth wobbles on its axis, and this wobble follows a seven-year pattern. The time of greatest wobble is a time of strong and frequent earthquakes. The Alaskan earthquake occurred in 1964, a year of maximum wobble. The Peruvian earthquake of 1970, taking the lives of more than 50,000 people, occurred when the wobble was approaching another peak. This phenomenon, however, does not explain the cause of continental drift.

Study of the mystery has opened a whole new field of geophysics. It is just one example of change that has come to science through the work of a few men chipping at the rocks of Antarctica.

Paleontology itself has been changed by Jensen's find. The fossil collectors had long failed to understand the limited diversity of reptiles as contrasted with the variety of mammals. The age of reptiles lasted 200 million years while the age of mammals started just 65 million years ago, yet there were only twenty orders of reptiles while thirty orders of mammals have already developed.

Continental drift now explains it. When reptiles dominated the earth, they shared one or nearly one land mass, and though the climate and forage varied with the latitudes, the differences were not as great as they are today. There was thus little need for great diversity among the reptiles. Mammals, however, developed when the continents were drifting apart. Species became specialized, evolving according to their varied foods and climate. The European horse, for instance, which reached the size of a rhinoceros, was less successful than the American horse and died out ten million years ago.

As we have seen, the American horse also died out, but not until after individuals had migrated across the Bering land bridge to Asia where the modern horse finally evolved.

Byrd and his companions, winging their way to the South Pole forty years before, never imagined that the bleak vista below would one day give man new understanding about the evolution of the horse.

The bones of penguins found in South America told of a similar branching of species. Except for the penguins of the Galapagos Islands off Ecuador, the South American penguins died out after Gondwanaland broke apart. The Antarctic penguins, able to adapt to the cold polar seas, survived.

The full potential of Antarctic research is just beginning to be appreciated. Studies range from air and ocean pollution to dating ice and tracking its movement. Some men want to learn of the minerals hidden in the ground. Others want to know the temperature of the stratosphere.

We know that pollution poses a dangerous threat to modern civilization, but we have learned only within the last few years that the best place to measure world pollution is on the barren Antarctic icecap. Here the carbon and sulfide compounds found by scientists give the most precise indication of world air pollution. The amount of impurity is not influenced by nearby factories or auto traffic. The increase in pollutants collected year by year in the Antarctic gives the true index for the increase in worldwide air pollution. Traces of the insecticide DDT have recently been found in penguins and seals. Scientists thus can sample the spreading pollution of the world's oceans. There are many warnings of doomsday coming from many sources, some more dramatic than valid, but the reports coming from Antarctica demand our concern.

Ice specialists still cannot agree on one of the most vital

Antarctic questions: Is the continent's icecap, holding more than 90 percent of the world's ice, shrinking or growing? The volume of ice has been calculated at 7,100,000 cubic miles, and we are told that if some cataclysm should melt it all, the oceans would rise 250 feet. Coastal cities would be inundated, and greater precipitation prompted by increased evaporation would probably make many regions of the world uninhabitable. Such an event seems highly unlikely, but even a slight change will alter coastlines and climate throughout the planet.

It was once thought that all ice moved slowly outward from the center of the continent in one, vast, spreading sheet, eventually returning to the sea the ice that fell as snow high on the plateau. However, scientists in the plateau stations operated by America and Russia have recorded surprisingly light snowfall, and the ice that forms from this snow is remarkably stable. Most of the ice in coastal glaciers and ice shelves, it turns out, originated from coastal snowstorms. Coastal winds influence the snow pack, and the number and size of snowstorms themselves vary from one season to the next. Though the balance of opinion today suggests that the Antarctic ice is increasing slightly, it will take years before the true trend is known.

One key to future ice conditions may be found in a study of the past. Cores through the polar ice may give a weather history of the world almost back to the Ice Age. Ice-coring is still an infant science, but researchers expect to learn a great deal about solar and cosmic radiation as well as meteorology from ice formed centuries ago. The deepest core so far was drilled by the Russians in 1971. The drill went 1,837 feet down, tapping ice 15,000 years old. Boris Kudryashov, who designed the drill, believes it is capable of going much deeper, perhaps to the bottom of the ice a mile and a quarter below the drilling station.

Less than 5 percent of the southern continent's bedrock is exposed, but explorers have already found greater deposits of coal than on any other continent. What further wealth lies beneath the ice? Perhaps it is too soon to talk of mining minerals in Antarctica, but when world demand justifies the expense, man will certainly find means to find and tap the remotest natural resources.

Studies of upper air currents and temperatures, aurora, magnetism, gravity, and weather similar to the studies conducted in the Arctic continue in Antarctica today. The coldest atmospheric temperature known to man was recorded by American scientists at the South Pole who sent up a weather balloon on July 16, 1958. At thirteen miles above the pole, the balloon's radio-rigged thermometer recorded $-135.4°$ F. Similar work with balloons disclosed a stable layer of air some 1,400 feet above the pole with temperatures of $-30°$ or $-40°$ F, much warmer than the surface air or the air above. The puzzling phenomenon is another subject for continuing study.

There are, in fact, so many research projects current and projected in the Antarctic that scientists themselves have difficulty keeping track. Little wonder Laurence M. Gould, who first went to the continent as second in command of Byrd's first expedition, recently called Antarctica the world's greatest laboratory.[17] It might never have reached this status without the impetus of the International Geophysical Year. Byrd lived long enough to help guide the start of this great undertaking.

16

Land of Peace

EARLY IN THE planning of IGY, world scientists agreed that the two major efforts of cooperative study should be outer space and Antarctica. The United States government saw the program as a chance to pick up where Highjump and Windmill left off.

Operation Deep Freeze, established to build and support IGY bases, would be mostly a navy project. Air force and army men and equipment would assist. Operation Deep Freeze continues to this day as do many of our IGY bases on Antarctica.

The icebreaker *Atka* went south early in 1955 to scout the coastline for landing sites and particularly to inspect the Bay of Whales and find if the nine DC3s left at Little America during Highjump were still usable. Men of the icebreaker found that a huge berg had broken from the ice shelf, carrying away all the planes and half the tent city. *Atka* skipper Glen Jacobsen decided Bay of Whales was no longer a safe harbor. He eventually picked Kainan Bay, fifty miles to the east, as the location for Little America V. Later in the season, *Atka* rounded the Antarctic Peninsula to survey possible harbors along Queen Maud Land. In addition to new charts and photos, *Atka* brought home fresh information on cosmic rays, upper air, and ocean currents. The voyage gave Byrd and other planners confidence in preparing for the next season.

By the time world scientists met in an IGY coordinating session in Rome during July of 1955, the United States had agreed to establish three Antarctic bases, one at Kainan Bay, another in Marie Byrd Land, and a third at the South Pole itself. However, the biggest news of the Rome session came from Russian scientists.

In earlier talk, it appeared that all IGY work by the Soviets would be conducted inside or close to Russian boundaries. The government of Moscow, following its old line, seemed reluctant to expose its men or its methods to the western world, but when delegates at Rome spoke of the need for a station at the South Geomagnetic Pole, the Russians said they intended to build one there. They would also build a station at the pole of inaccessibility. The South Geomagnetic Pole, high on the Antarctic plateau, marks the spot where the lines of magnetic force surrounding the earth converge.

The pole of inaccessibility is simply a spot which is the greatest distance from the coast in all directions. The Russians would build a coastal station near the Shackleton Ice Shelf and send tractor caravans inland to establish the two polar stations.

For a time, the announcement made the Australian public uneasy. This would be within the territory the Australians claimed, but most scientists hailed the Soviet entry as a boon to science. Today, observers of world politics look upon the Rome announcement as the first development in thawing the Cold War between East and West.

The announcement sparked IGY with a competitive spirit. The United States planners decided to increase the number of its bases. Added would be an air station at McMurdo Sound, another in Vincennes Bay to be known as Wilkes Station, and a third on the Filchner Ice Shelf in the Weddell Sea to be known as Ellsworth Station.

In December of 1955 seven separate expeditions sailed for Antarctica to prepare one of the greatest peaceful assaults ever launched by man. Our Deep Freeze expedition included 1,800 men and seven ships. For the first time, planes would be flown across the Southern Ocean to Antarctica. On December 20, soon after a landing strip at McMurdo Station was completed, four big planes arrived from New Zealand. Within a month, these planes began ranging far over Antarctica. One reached the Weddell Sea and surveyed a region the British would enter at the start of their proposed Commonwealth Trans-Antarctic Expedition. Another flight reached the coast of the Davis Sea where the Russians were soon expected. In all, nine flights, covering 23,000 miles, were crowded into two days of good flying weather.

One problem emerging from these long-range flights was the exceptional height of the polar plateau. With the maximum elevation at 14,000, the plateau forced the planes to the limit of their ceiling. If one should be forced down, the engines would not generate enough power for takeoff in the thin air of such altitudes. Fortunately, the flights were made without a hitch, and Byrd had the satisfaction of sending a note to the Russians, reporting on conditions in their region, and saying in effect that the United States Navy had beaten them to their chosen region.

Meanwhile, at Kainan Bay, men worked quickly to establish Little America V. Seventeen prefabricated houses were erected there, and 550 tons of supplies and equipment needed for Byrd Station, to be built 600 miles inland, were unloaded and stored for the next season. At McMurdo men unloaded 4,000 tons of cargo from the ships. Some of it would serve McMurdo Station. The rest would be airlifted to the South Pole for the IGY station there. Two big barges, carrying a total of 500,000 gallons of fuel, were docked close to the base and left to be frozen in winter ice.

In March 1956, with the southern summer nearly over, the ships retreated, leaving seventy-three men to winter at Little America and ninety-three at McMurdo Station. Deep Freeze commander George Dufek, in the powerful new icebreaker *Glacier,* used the last few weeks of the season to cruise around to the opposite side of the continent and make three landings on the coast of Queen Maud Land. The Stars and Stripes were raised at each landing site.

During the same season that the Americans built their bases, other nations made similar preparations. Chile, Argentina, Australia, and England, all with stations already established on the continent, had an easier job than other countries. Often new equipment and some expansion of facilities were all that was necessary to prepare for IGY. England, however, added two new stations off the coast of the Weddell Sea in the 1955–56 season. One was a station for the Royal Society Expedition. The other was base for the Commonwealth Trans-Antarctic Expedition to be led by Vivian (later Sir Vivian) Fuchs. Fuchs and his men would try for the goal Filchner and Shackleton had failed to attain. The crossing project was criticized by some British scientists as a stunt, but as it turned out, the crossing proved scientifically productive. The Royal Society camp was established at Halley Bay while Fuchs and his men put their base to the southwest at the edge of the Filchner Ice Shelf. They named it Shackleton.

At McMurdo Sound, meanwhile, New Zealanders under Sir Edmund Hillary, conqueror of Mount Everest, set up base near the American station. Hillary and his men would climb through the mountains to the west, reach the plateau, and connect with Fuchs the following season. New Zealand also staffed Hallett Station near Cape Adare, a station built for IGY by the United States.

The French reactivated their outpost on the Adelie Coast. Australians beefed up their existing bases, including Mawson Station on the MacRobertson Coast, facing the heart of the Indian Ocean.

The Russians established their camp between the French and Australians on the shore of the Davis Sea. They called it Mirny, the Russian word for peace. To supply inland outposts, the Russians would rely on heavy tractors and cargo sledges for transport. Elevations, the Russians decided, were too great for safe airlift. During the 1955–56 season, Mikhail M. Somov, commander of the expedition, led a tractor caravan inland. Thick snow made travel extremely difficult, and the disappointed Russians finally had to settle for a small station just 230 miles from the coast. They called it Pionerskaya. The men left to man it became the first to camp on the Antarctic Plateau through a winter.

Late in 1956, with the return of the sun to the high latitudes, work began anew all around the continent. For Operation Deep Freeze, the biggest challenge was establishing the station at the South Pole. Everything—food, fuel, power plants, prefabricated houses, and scientific gear—had to be flown in from McMurdo Station. The first step was the construction of a refueling station at the base of Liv Glacier, where the Douglas ski planes could stop on their return from the pole. This station would provide weather reports for the flights and serve, if needed, as a base for rescue operations.

On October 31, 1956, two days after the fueling station was established, a plane took Dufek to the South Pole. He became the first to set foot there since the Amundsen and Scott expeditions forty-two years earlier. The temperature was —58° F, and Dufek decided to delay the airlift until the weather turned warmer. His plane needed all jet boosters to lift clear of the ice.

On November 20, a reconnaissance party of eight men and eleven sledge dogs was landed at the pole by two Douglas ski planes. Big Globemasters, circling overhead, parachuted the first shipments of cargo.

Lieutenant (j.g.) Richard A. Bowers, commander of the party, determined through sun shots that the South Pole was actually nine miles away. The men gathered up what gear they could haul and carry and marched to the goal behind a team of pulling dogs. It did not seem that exploration had changed much since Amundsen's day, but soon after initial camp was established, the sky began to throb with circling aircraft and supplies rained down upon the ice. More men, including Paul Siple, arrived. He would head scientific operations.

The remote outpost was christened the Amundsen-Scott IGY South Pole Station. At 9,200-feet altitude, the thin air made heavy work difficult and extremely tiring. Simply breathing the cold air burned up extra body energy. All men lost weight. Siple, at 250 pounds the biggest man in the party, lost thirty-nine pounds during the construction of the station.

The biggest worry for the men was fire. If their buildings were destroyed during the winter, they would be turned out in the night with no shelter and no hope of rescue. The men built their camp in two sections divided by a wall of snow. Enough food for survival was stored on either side. In addition a hut set up two hundred feet away held sleeping bags, emergency food, and rations.

Air Force Globemasters of the 63rd Troop Carrier Group continued to drop supplies throughout the flying season. By February 21, 1957, after sixty-five separate missions, 760 tons of cargo had been delivered to the South Pole. It has been estimated that it cost one million dollars per man to establish the eighteen-man polar station. An expensive operation indeed, but it was accomplished without serious accident or injury.

On March 12, not long after the last plane vanished over the northern horizon, the station radioman tuned in on an

Armed Forces Radio news broadcast and learned of the death
in Boston that day of Admiral Byrd. For Siple, the news was
particularly depressing.[18] At 69, Byrd's failing health had
kept him from coming to the Antarctic for the start of IGY,
but his guidance had continued during preparations. Byrd,
in fact, had recommended Siple for the South Pole command. Siple knew better than anyone else that the great
venture ahead would have been impossible if it were not for
Byrd's life-long dedication to discovery.

Soon after the sad news spread through the station, one of
the men offered to lower the Stars and Stripes to half staff.
No, Siple said, he would do that himself. America had lost
a leading citizen, but Siple, who had been on every expedition Byrd led to Antarctica, had lost his best friend.

The wind-tattered flag flew for ten days. Then it was time
to take it down. The polar night had begun.

Perhaps the greatest testament to Byrd was the roster of
American leaders in the Antarctic during IGY. Other than
Siple and Dufek, the list included Finn Ronne, in charge of
Ellsworth Station; Carl Eklund, scientific leader at Wilkes
Station, and Laurence M. Gould, over-all director of the
United States Antarctic Program. These men had all gained
their Antarctic experience under Byrd. There were many
others.

During the rush to prepare the South Pole station for the
long night, a tractor caravan set out from Little America V
with the cargo for Byrd Station. The journey proved to be
one of the most hazardous ventures of the entire American
program because the region where the ice of Marie Byrd
Land oozed down to meet the Ross Ice Shelf was a mass of
crevasses. Progress stopped as army ice experts leading the

caravan sent out survey parties to find safe passage. The big Diesel tractors and their cargo sleds weighed fifty tons each, enough to break down most snow bridges that roofed many crevasses. Eventually a route was found running along the ridges between crevasses, but there were still many pitfalls that had to be packed with snow before the big vehicles could pass.

It took five weeks to lay the 650-mile trail to the site for the station. Then cargo caravans began to roll and their deliveries, along with 240 tons delivered by air force planes, enabled work at the new station to be completed before winter. Twenty-two men, including twelve scientists, were left to staff Byrd Station.

For to the west, almost opposite Byrd Station, Soviet tractor parties worked inland, struggling through thick snow to reach the pole of inaccessibility and the geomagnetic pole. The snow mounded up ahead of tractors and sleds. As the machines climbed higher, they lost power in the thin air. It was humiliating, but the Soviets were forced to stop short of their goals again. On March 30, 1957, they set up a station almost four hundred miles short of the geomagnetic pole. Meanwhile, Soviet engineers at home worked feverishly to improve the design of their snow tractors for the next summer.

In October the new assault began. Planes established a fuel dump 530 miles inland at a station christened Komsomolskaya, 11,400 feet above sea level. Here one caravan turned left toward the geomagnetic pole and another turned right toward the pole of inaccessibility. Alexei Treshnikov, who had replaced Somov as head of the Russian expedition, led the geomagnetic pole party to its goal December 16. The pole of inaccessibility party, led by Vitali K. Babarykin,

mired in the deepest snow yet. Tracks sank five feet. Even
with superchargers, the engines lacked the strength to move
the heavy sleds at anything faster than a crawl. At twelve
thousand feet altitude, the men grew weak, gasping pain-
fully in the subzero air. Babarykin stopped and set up his
station four hundred miles short of his goal. His outpost was
christened Sovietskaya, and five men were left to man it.
Treshnikov's camp was named Vostok. It was staffed for the
winter with eleven men.

The men at Sovietskaya suffered headaches, pounding
hearts, and low blood pressure, but they performed their
duties despite extreme cold and an altitude of 12,280 feet.
Water boiled at such a low temperature at this altitude that
it was difficult to cook food. The men lost weight. At Vostok
the thermometer showed $-125.3°$ F. Temperatures at Sovietskaya, at a higher altitude than Vostok, were even lower, but
the thermometer there was not calibrated for such readings.

At both stations, men carried battery-powered heaters
under their clothing when they went outside. Before going
out, they rigged breathing hoses from face masks to a spot
near the heaters beneath their clothing. In this way, they
prevented ice-crystal damage to their throats and lungs from
direct breathing of the cold air.

Strange phenomena occurred in the extreme cold. Water
dropped on the ice danced as if tossed on a hot stove before
it froze into pearl-like droplets. Kerosene left outside turned
to something that looked like wet snow. Ink in the pens of
the recording devices for the instruments froze, even after
the ink was mixed with antifreeze. Surprisingly, during the
extreme cold, the temperature six to eight feet up was five
degrees warmer than at ground level.

The air remained calm through most of the winter at the Soviet inland stations, but back at Pionerskaya, blizzards roared about the huts almost daily. Snow caved in tunnels and the roofs of some buildings, and the men had to struggle with shoring timbers to keep the shelters from collapsing completely under the growing pack. By contrast, the annual accumulation of snow high on the plateau was ten inches and less.

Late in 1958, the Russians tried once more for the pole of inaccessibility. It took fifty-two days to cover the 1,360 miles, but the men won the goal just two weeks before the end of IGY. On these and other overland expeditions, the Soviets made frequent soundings to measure the thickness of the ice which showed that the Antarctic ice in the region covered a rock foundation well above sea level. The soundings also revealed a huge valley leading to the Amery Ice Shelf and Prydz Bay. The river of ice filling this valley proved to be at least two hundred miles long, making it the world's biggest glacier. The Soviets named the discovery IGY Valley. The Russians made dozens of coastal landings and established a satellite station at Bunger Hills where the winds were so strong they blew away, almost at once, all snow that fell.

Among the Russian's many fields of study was the test of a theory that ocean currents caused electrical currents which influence magnetic variation. Along the coast of the continent where currents were greatest, scientists found variation greater than inland and out to sea. This did not prove the theory, but it gave it firm support.

West of the Russians, thick snow delayed the Australians in their efforts to work inland. Several journeys were completed, however, and many soundings were taken through the ice. Scientists based at Mawson Station made a special study of ice flow, and found that some streams of ice moved toward the sea three feet a day. Surrounding ice of the plateau, however, crept at only 1.6 inches daily. During IGY, the Australians opened a second station in the Vestfold Hills between Mirny and Mawson. They also made numerous landings along the coast and discovered iron ore in some regions.

Japanese scientists, meanwhile, operated out of a station on Lützow-Holm Bay west of Mawson. Sea ice delayed the start of work there, and the Japanese, operating without an ice-breaker, had to call for help. The Russian icebreaker *Ob* went to the rescue. But trouble continued for the Japanese. A berg broke from shore and carried away six tons of supplies. Later a hut burned with the loss of scientific records. Then, after the first winter, ice blocked a relief ship from reaching the shore station. It was finally necessary to airlift the men out before the end of IGY.

Farther west still, the Belgians established a station in Queen Maud Land. They too had difficulties. The expedition was led by Gaston de Gerlache de Gomery, son of Adrien de Gerlache, commander of Belgium's first expedition to Antarctica more than a half century earlier. The Belgian IGY expedition consisted of seventeen men, one plane, a helicopter, twenty-four dogs, and two Sno-cats. Near the end of IGY de Gerlache took off in the single engine plane with three others and failed to return.

The Russians, one quarter of the way around the continent to the east, were the first to respond to the call for help. V. M. Perov, Mirny's chief aviator, took off, stopped at Mawson to refuel and arrived at the Belgian base to begin a series of search flights. Perov spotted the wreckage of the missing plane in the Crystal Mountains near the coast. He landed and found a note. De Gerlache and his companions had started walking toward a supply depot eighty miles away. The Russian pilot took off and followed the path he assumed the Belgians had taken. Soon he sighted four specks creeping slowly across the ice. Rescue was swiftly accomplished, and Perov later received the Order of Leopold I from a thankful Belgian government.

Norwegian explorers for IGY, based west of the Belgians, worked inland toward mountains some one hundred and fifty miles from the coast, but crevassed ice forced the men to turn back sooner than hoped. Scientists, however, collected important weather and aurora observations in a region where little information had been obtained before. The same was true of work done by English, Argentine, and American scientists along the coast of the Weddell Sea.

All weather data collected by the IGY stations went to a clearing house at Little America V where meteorologists finally were able to discern a pattern of Antarctic weather. The maps of storms drawn up in Weather Central, as the clearing house was called, showed that cyclonic storms moved around the continent from west to east, and while small storms hugged the coast, the major disturbances swung far out to sea. Temperature readings produced some surprises. While men on the plateau were recording their record lows, those in coastal stations often enjoyed balmy weather, balmy at least for the Antarctic. Vostok had a mean temperature of $-67.7°$ F for 1958 while Wilkes Station had a mean of 21.7° F. Men at Wilkes Station, in fact, had a milder winter that year than residents of Nebraska.

During IGY, sixteen trail parties representing eight different nations worked out from various bases to traverse portions of the continent, map surface features, and sound the thickness of the ice. In all, the trail parties covered fourteen thousand miles. Men working out from Byrd Station found most of the rock foundation of Marie Byrd Land lay below sea level. Close to Byrd Station, the ice was fourteen thousand feet thick. No soundings since have found thicker ice.

A trail party from Ellsworth Station discovered that the Filchner Ice Shelf was much larger than charts showed. Map makers have since added an area equal to that of Lake Superior to the Weddell Sea, an area previously thought part of the continent. In the middle of the ice shelf IGY explorers found a dome of ice shoved up by a large island. The trail party crossed it, continued to the Dufek Massive, and found snow-free regions among the peaks. The following season, actually after IGY had ended, another trail party from Ellsworth marched to Byrd Station and onto the Ross Sea. It found deep ice with foundations below sea level in many areas, but a mountain range hidden beneath the ice separated the Ross and Weddell seas.

The most publicized traverse of IGY was actually not part of the IGY program. The Commonwealth Trans-Antarctic Expedition traveled 2,180 miles from the Weddell Sea to the Ross Sea by way of the pole in ninety-nine days. Seismic shots, made every thirty miles, showed land beneath the ice stood above sea level except near the coasts. Though the British found 8,000-foot-thick ice at the South Pole itself, echoes twenty-five miles on either side bounced back quickly, indicating submerged mountains rising to within 2,000 feet of the surface.

Fuchs and his men were much delayed by rough ice soon after leaving Shackleton, and Hillary, working in from the

McMurdo side, radioed to suggest that the crossing party stop at the pole and resume next season. Fuchs declined and continued, but four days after saying goodbye to Americans at Amundsen-Scott Station, Fuchs needed help. One of his men had been overcome by engine fumes. The man regained consciousness, but oxygen was needed to revive him fully. This was brought out and parachuted to the trail party by two navy planes from McMurdo Station. Fuchs pressed on and soon met Hillary and his New Zealanders. Together the two parties marched to McMurdo Sound, arriving there on March 2, 1958. The British public gloried in the achievement. It seemed to cure the old pains of Scott's loss and Shackleton's failure.

Most IGY trail parties carried gravity instruments, and findings of scientists showed that the continent was in equilibrium. The land, in other words, had subsided as far as it would beneath the huge weight of ice. If the ice were removed, the continent would rise like a ship relieved of its cargo. On the Indian Ocean side, Russians figured the land would come up 250 feet. Americans in Marie Byrd Land figured the rise there would be closer to 1,600 feet.

Unfortunately, the great achievements of IGY were not attained without losses. Four U.S. Navy men were killed when their plane crashed in a landing attempt during poor visibility at McMurdo Station. Later, six men died when a Globemaster crashed while making an air drop at Hallett Station. McMurdo and Little America each lost a tractor driver through the ice. The Russians also lost a tractor driver at Mirny, and two Russians were lost when a berg crashed from an ice shelf onto the deck of a ship while crews were unloading cargo. The greatest tragedy was suffered by Argentina. The naval vessel *Guarian,* hurrying to the aid of a sick man in an Argentine station, sank with the loss of thirty-six lives.

The losses, in many cases, could be blamed on inexperience. The year-round population of Antarctica, after all, had jumped from 179 to 912 at the start of IGY, and the summer influx of scientists and workers brought the total population close to 5,000. There were bound to be accidents.

Scientists are still working with data collected in Antarctica during IGY. It is impossible to measure the full value of such data, but nearly all scientists today agree that the greatest single event of IGY in the Antarctic in terms of man's efforts to learn more about earth, was the decision to continue cooperative research. While the "year" was still in progress, United States scientists urged that all nations consider a continuance in the Antarctic. The International Conference of Scientific Unions, coordinating all IGY work, created SCAR (Special Committee on Antarctic Research). It continues to function today, coordinating work of thirty Antarctic bases.

There have been many changes since IGY. The United States, for instance, has closed its Little America, Ellsworth, and Hallett stations. Australia has taken over Wilkes Station. New stations, however, have been created. Palmer Station on Anvers Island off the west coast of the Antarctic Peninsula and Eights Station, in the interior where the peninsula joins the continent, are two of our major additions. We continue to operate McMurdo, Byrd, and Amundsen-Scott Stations. All continue to receive support from Deep Freeze.

Each summer, workers and scientists arrive on flights from New Zealand. The scientists, such as the paleontologists who dug fossils at Coalsack Bluff, all have well-planned programs of research drawn up long before arrival on the southern continent. The navy men of Deep Freeze set up and supply temporary camps or run tractor traverses across the ice as needed to support research. Each summer, navy crews repair and restock the stations, readying them for another winter. Those who served through the previous winter are flown home, while staffs of new navy specialists and scientists are installed for the winter to come.

McMurdo is headquarters for all our Antarctic stations. Here supplies and men arrive on huge C-130 Hercules cargo planes manned by volunteer navy crews. The landing field is on packed ice, but McMurdo Station itself stands on the southern slope of Ross Island. Two-story steel buildings have recently replaced the prefabricated huts and barracks of IGY.

The station gets both its power and water supply from an atomic reactor. The portable nuclear plant takes water from the Ross Sea, pumps it, purifies, and distills it. The distilled water is then fed through pipes and turned to steam by nuclear fission. The steam goes to a turbine which turns the plant's 1500-kilowatt generator. The steam is also used to pump more water from the sea and distill it for the station drinking water. Spent steam is condensed for reuse. Many believe that the atomic plant at McMurdo will solve the expensive fuel supply and fresh water problems in Antarctica, but other United States stations still get power and heat to melt ice from conventional fuels.

America's second most important base in Antarctica is Byrd Station, 835 miles east of McMurdo and 600 miles from the South Pole. It is a small city beneath the ice with space for many more than the staff of thirty-six that now spends the winter there. In 1961 the original station was replaced. Five huge ditches, twenty-eight feet wide and up to 1,600 feet long, were gouged into the snow and ice. Buildings were erected and then the ditches were roofed over and buried in snow. The snow cover today is thirty feet thick. On the surface, all that marks the station is a radar dome, a box-like house for aurora observations, and a platform for launching weather balloons. In winter, men leave the tunnels only to maintain and read outside instruments. When the temperature dips to —80° F, few are anxious to perform these chores.

Scott-Amundsen Station, as it is now called, is also under ice with little to mark the South Pole but the shelters for observatories and weather instruments. Below the ice, however, the polar station is much smaller than Byrd. The tunnels are only seven feet high, and workers each summer must strengthen the roof timbers and replace buckling oil drums and packing crates that support them. The window-less buildings within these passages house a winter crew of nineteen or twenty men. Tunnels fan out from the station beneath the ice, leading to seismic instruments that record earthquakes originating from any region on earth. Other instruments record magnetic variation. One chamber, lined with lead to shield out local radiation, measures cosmic rays. There is even a tunnel going ninety feet straight down at the pole. Scientists once used it to study the age of ice. Today it serves as a mine for collecting ice to be melted for the base water supply.

Eights Station, built in 1962 in less than a month, is one of the smallest and most comfortable of all United States outposts in Antarctica. It too is buried beneath the snow, but its buildings consist of eight well-insulated, waterproof units little different from house trailers. These units, eight feet wide, eight feet tall, and twenty-seven feet long, were carried to the station by C-130 Hercules cargo planes from Mc-Murdo, 1,578 miles away. The units are joined by a corridor that doubles as a common room for the staff of eleven men. The main purpose of Eights Station is upper air research. It was named for James Eights of Albany, New York, a scientist who came to the Antarctic with Wilkes in 1830.

Palmer Station, built in 1965, houses nine men for winter research. All these stations are completely isolated for more than six months of the year. Men receive no mail, and are lucky if a radio amateur can connect them by telephone patch with relatives in America. Such connections are often more frustrating than rewarding, for the radio signal has a way of fading soon after relay of conversation begins.

During the Antarctic night, men get to know each other very well. There are few disagreements. Ability to get along with others is a characteristic needed in qualifying for polar duty, and there is something about living on the world's remotest continent that brings men together. Friendship, loyalty, and companionship become bywords. Another important word is home. Wintering crews look forward eagerly to the first plane of the summer with letters from home, fresh news, and a new supply of films.

There are stories told of men who have watched a movie so many times they run it backwards for variety. On other occasions, a film has been shown with the sound turned off. Men have seen it so often they know the dialogue by heart, and each man speaks a role, usually with comic alteration of the original.

Russia maintains bases at Mirny, Komsomolskaya, and Vostok and has added two coastal bases in Queen Maud Land. Argentina, Chile, and England continue to man bases on the Antarctic Peninsula. Australia, France, and Belgium operate the stations they activated for IGY.

Nearly all nations represented on the southern continent

exchange scientists. An American scientist works with Russian colleagues at Mirny, while a Russian works at McMurdo with American counterparts. Though language differences create some difficulty in the early weeks, the scientists are soon exchanging information freely, breaking through both political and language barriers.

Except for the peninsula dispute and fights among early sealers, peace has been the rule in Antarctica. Cooperation becomes far more important there than political ideology. Companionship means more than national competition.

Western suspicion and fear of Russia slackened almost from the beginning of the IGY venture. The Russians seemed just as anxious to cooperate and assist as anyone else. Their response to calls for help from Antarctic neighbors was impressive for its promptness and good spirit. IGY participants took note of this good spirit that seemed universal in the southern continent. Could it be preserved in some way?

The question prompted President Eisenhower to call a conference in Washington. Delegates from participating countries started discussion of a pact on May 3, 1958, seven months before the end of IGY. From this and other meetings came the Antarctic Treaty unique in history, and one that could guide mankind to world peace.

The treaty sets aside a large part of the world, its fifth largest continent, for peaceful use. No weapons, no fortification, no military maneuvers can be considered. No nuclear devices can be exploded. The treaty also establishes a free inspection system to assure compliance. It preserves Antarctica for research by scientists of any nation.

The document was signed by representatives of sixteen

nations on December 1, 1959. It went into force in 1961. The nations are Argentina, Australia, Belgium, Chile, Czechoslovakia, Denmark, France, Japan, the Netherlands, New Zealand, Norway, Poland, South Africa, the Soviet Union, the United Kingdom, and the United States. All have respected the agreement without exception.

The Antarctic Treaty has been a precedent for other steps toward peace, including the nuclear test ban treaty of 1963, the space compact of 1967, and the nuclear nonproliferation pact of 1968. The southern continent has thus become a laboratory for political as well as natural science.

On December 1, 1969, the signing nations marked the tenth anniversary of the Antarctic Treaty. Probably the most moving observation was held at McMurdo Sound. Polar veteran Laurence Gould was there. On the eve of the event, Americans held a simple ceremony before the statue of Admiral Byrd which stands at McMurdo Station. Next day, representatives of all SCAR nations gathered at nearby Scott Station, operated by New Zealand. The sixteen flags of the signing nations flew over the base as brief speeches were given by each delegate. Gould reported that the hope for peace expressed by the Soviet representative was among the most eloquent.

Man must dedicate all efforts to make the hope voiced at a distant frontier become a reality throughout the world. Here is the great challenge for this and future generations. It is a greater, more complex challenge than any faced by polar explorers. If man fails, then mankind is doomed, but if he rises to the challenge, then mankind rises to the greatest venture yet.

Notes

1. *Exploring Ocean Frontiers: A Background Book on Who Owns the Seas* by Frances and Walter Scott, Parents' Magazine Press, New York, 1970.

2. "A Stone Age Campsite at the Gateway to America" by Douglas D. Anderson, *Scientific American,* New York, June, 1968.

3. *Ancient Cultures of the Bering Sea and the Eskimo Problem* by S. I. Rudenko, translated by Paul Tolstoy, University of Toronto Press, Toronto, 1961.

4. *Peter Freuchen's Book of Eskimos* by Peter Freuchen, World Publishing Company, Cleveland and New York, 1961.

5. *The Northwest Passage* by Roald Amundsen, E. P. Dutton, New York, 1908.

6. *People of the Deer* by Farley Mowat, Little, Brown, Boston and Toronto, 1952.

7. *Unsolved Mysteries of the Arctic* by Vilhjalmur Stefansson, Macmillan, New York, 1940.

8. *The Northwest Passage* by Roald Amundsen, E. P. Dutton, New York, 1908.

9. *Farthest North* by Fridtjof Nansen, in two volumes, Harper, New York, 1897.

10. *My Life as an Explorer* by Roald Amundsen, Doubleday, Page, Garden City, New York, 1927.

11. "Polar Bear: Lonely Nomad of the North" by Thor Larsen, *National Geographic,* Washington, D. C., April, 1971.

12. "The Shifting World of Arctic Ice" by Louise Purrett, *Science News,* Washington, D. C., July 31, 1971.

13. *Quest for a Continent: The Story of the Antarctic* by Walter Sullivan, McGraw-Hill, New York, 1957.

14. "The End of the Big Blubber," *Time,* New York, November 29, 1968.

15. "The World of Antarctic Paleontology" and "Horizons for Antarctic Paleontology" by Kendrick Frazier, *Science News,* Washington, D. C., March 28 and April 4, 1970.

16. *Our Wandering Continents* by A. L. du Toit, Oliver and Boyd, Ltd., London, 1937.

17. "Antarctica: The World's Greatest Laboratory" by Laurence M. Gould, *American Scholar,* Washington, D. C., Summer, 1971.

18. *90° South* by Paul Siple, Putnam, New York, 1959.

Bibliography

Anderson, William R., with Clay Blair, Jr., *Nautilus 90 North*, New American Library, New York, 1959.

Ash, Christopher, *Whaler's Eye*, Macmillan, New York, 1962.

Baum, Allyn, *Antarctica: The Worst Place in the World*, Macmillan, New York, 1966.

Blond, Georges, *The Great Story of Whales*, translated from the French by James Cleugh, Hanover House, Garden City, New York, 1955.

Brontman, Lazar, *On Top of the World: The Soviet Expedition to the North Pole, 1937–1938*, Covici Friede, New York, 1938.

Byrd, Richard E., *Little America, Aerial Exploration in the Antarctic, the Flight to the South Pole*, Putnam, New York, 1930.

Byrd, Richard E., *Skyward,* Putnam, New York, 1928.

Church, Albert Cook, *Whale Ships and Whaling,* Bonanza Books, New York, 1938.

Dolan, Edward F., Jr., *White Battleground: The Conquest of the Arctic,* Dodd, Mead, New York, 1961.

Dyson, James L., *The World of Ice,* Knopf, New York, 1962.

Ellsberg, Edward, *Hell on Ice: The Saga of the "Jeannette,"* Dodd, Mead, New York, 1938.

Freuchen, Peter, *Peter Freuchen's Book of Eskimos,* World Publishing Company, Cleveland, 1961.

Garfield, Brian, *The Thousand Mile War: World War II in Alaska and the Aleutians,* Ballantine Books, New York, 1969.

Giddings, Louis J., Jr., *Ancient Men of the Arctic,* Knopf, New York, 1967.

Gregory, James S., *Russian Land, Soviet People,* Pegasus, New York, 1968.

Grierson, John, *Challenge to the Poles, Highlights of Arctic and Antarctic Aviation,* Archon Books, Hamden, Conn., 1964.

Hardy, Sir Alister, *Great Waters,* Harper, New York, 1967.

Howland, Chester, *Thar She Blows!,* Wilfred Funk, New York, 1951.

Jenness, Diamond, *The People of the Twilight,* University of Chicago Press, Chicago, 1928.

Keating, Bern, *Alaska,* National Geographic Society, Washington, D. C., 1969.

Lansing, Alfred, *Endurance, Shackleton's Incredible Voyage,* McGraw-Hill, New York, 1959.

Ley, Willy, and the editors of Time-Life Books, *The Poles,* Time-Life Books, New York, 1962.

Maxwell, Gavin, *Seals of the World,* Houghton Mifflin, Boston, 1967.

Members of the expedition: *The Voyage of the Chelyuskin,* translated by Alec Brown, Macmillan, New York, 1935.

Mowat, Farley, *Canada North,* Little, Brown, Boston, 1967.

Mowat, Farley, *People of the Deer,* Little, Brown, Boston, 1952.

Murphy, Robert, *The Haunted Journey,* Doubleday, Garden City, New York, 1961.

Nansen, Dr. Fridtjof, *Farthest North,* Harper, New York, 1898.

Neatby, Leslie H., *In Quest of the Northwest Passage,* Thomas Y. Crowell, New York, 1958.

Peary, Robert E., *The North Pole: Its Discovery in 1909 under the Auspices of the Peary Arctic Club,* Frederick A. Stokes, New York, 1910.

Pedersen, Alwin, *Polar Animals,* translated from the French by Gwynne Vevers, Taplinger, New York, 1966.

Perry, Richard, *The World of the Walrus,* Taplinger, New York, 1968.

Rodahl, Kaare, *North: The Nature and Drama of the Polar World,* Harper, New York, 1953.

Scheffer, Victor B., *The Year of the Whale,* Scribner's, New York, 1969.

Semyonov, Yuri, *Siberia, Its Conquest and Development,* translated by J. R. Foster, Helicon Press, Inc., Baltimore, 1963.

Stefansson, Vilhjalmur, *Ultima Thule, Further Mysteries of the Arctic,* Macmillan, New York, 1940.

Stefansson, Vilhjalmur, *Unsolved Mysteries of the Arctic,* Macmillan, New York, 1940.

St. George, George, *Siberia, the New Frontier,* McKay, New York, 1969.

Sullivan, Walter, *Assault on the Unknown,* McGraw-Hill, New York, 1961.

Sullivan, Walter, *Quest for a Continent: The Story of the Antarctic,* McGraw-Hill, New York, 1957.

Sutton, George Miksch, *High Arctic: An Expedition to the Unspoiled North,* Paul S. Eriksson, New York, 1971.

Thorén, Ragnar, *Picture Atlas of the Arctic,* Elsevier, Amsterdam, Netherlands, 1969.

Vandercook, John W., *Great Sailor: A Life of the Discoverer, Captain James Cook,* Dial, New York, 1951.

Weyer, Edward Moffat, *The Eskimos, Their Environment and Folkways,* Archon Books, Hamden, Conn., 1969 (First published by Yale University Press, New Haven, 1932).

Wilkins, Capt. George H., *Flying the Arctic,* Grosset and Dunlap, New York, 1928.

Index